EVEN
GREATER

REINHARD BONNKE

54
86

EVEN
GREATER

12 REAL-LIFE STORIES *that* INSPIRE
YOU *to* DO GREAT THINGS *for* GOD

Editor: S.K. Tomazsewski
Cover Design: Bill Chiaravalle/Brand Navigation
Typeset: Adrian Bradshaw

Published by Full Flame, LLC
P. O. Box 593647
Orlando, FL 32859
USA

www.FullFlameOnline.com

Printed in the USA

CONTENTS

FOREWORD

The privilege of writing a foreword to an author's book is that the author is defenseless against your words. That's why I have the liberty of saying what follows, knowing full well that if my friend Reinhard Bonnke saw my words before they appeared in print he would not allow them. Now, here's what I have to say, unchallenged by the evangelist himself.

> *I believe that honesty requires acknowledging that Reinhard Bonnke is the most far-reaching, most dynamically penetrating international evangelist in the world. The raw statistics, not only of millions of souls brought to Christ over the past quarter century, but the thousands of churches born, or dramatically expanded with surging growth, testify to the viability of my assertion.*

As true as I believe the above assessment to be, I am not stating it to propose a competition between reputations, or to trivialize the great achievements of many other remarkably great leaders the Holy Spirit has used in the present generation. But for leading the way in demonstrating the simple power of first century Christianity in the 20th century and into the 21st, there is an unmatchable record of miracle grace and power that has left a trail of holy fire wherever Reinhard has gone – throughout all of Africa, as well as in other pagan strongholds of the world.

I am neither given to flattery nor exaggeration, but have simply seen too much of the fire of God's Spirit at work in Reinhard Bonnke's crusades, and heard too many reports of the fruit of God's eternal workings remaining after the crusades are past. By this kind of fruit, the kind that lasts, born of a ministry that is filled with integrity, holiness of life and driven by a non-self-serving zeal for souls like I have never seen in another person – by this kind of fruit, Jesus said, we shall *know* true servants of the Gospel.

In this book, the evangelist tells some of the miracle stories that have distilled from crusades. Some of these crusades have numbered more than a million people in a single service, and it is common (if such a word is fitting for such miracles) that more than 100,000 souls will confess Christ at a single event!

My suggestion regarding Reinhard Bonnke's uniqueness in our time might be challenged by some. I understand, for I know other remarkable and great leaders, both living as well as now-in-glory, and it is difficult to measure ministry. But in any case, without trumpeting a ministry for the sake of fame, but simply because of the results in his proclaiming "The Name Jesus", the Name above all, I invite you to settle in with this book.

You'll not be the same after you read it, because here are stories of the Holy Spirit at work, glorifying Jesus at every turn, transforming, healing and delivering souls into Christ's wonderful life and glory.

They're told by one of His servants. I think you'll enjoy meeting him too, and learning why he is so effective at introducing people to the dear Savior – The Lord Jesus Christ.

Jack W. Hayford, Chancellor
The King's Seminary
Los Angeles, California

INTRODUCTION

AGENTS OF OMNIPOTENCE

I am Reinhard Bonnke, an evangelist. You might have heard of my crusades. Or maybe not. It doesn't matter. I want you to stand next to me.

You may not want to do that. You may not like the idea that I am an evangelist. My name may sound strange to you. When I speak English, some people are put off by my German accent. You may not agree with my church background or beliefs. It doesn't matter. I want you to stand next to me on a great outdoor stage as people are gathering around us from every direction.

I want you so close that I can put my arm around your shoulder. I want you to sense the excitement rushing through my veins. You should stand near enough to hear me breathing. Why? Because I want you to know for sure that I am human, just like you. I want you to know that what has happened to me can happen to you.

That is why we stand together on this platform. On this night we see something that perhaps no eye has seen in the history of the world. The crowd has gathered, and we look across a sea of faces that stretches to the horizon. It is a crowd of 1,600,000 people!

Can you comprehend a crowd so big? There is no church or cathedral large enough to hold a fraction of them. No city on earth has a sports stadium big enough to house even a small portion of them. The people are gathered in a vast open space that forms a natural amphitheater in front of us, so that we can see them, and they can see us. They are standing, not sitting.

We are looking at more than three times the number of people that came to the famous Woodstock Music Festival in America in 1969. Woodstock changed a generation, but this crowd makes Woodstock look small. Think of how much the world might change if this many people come to Jesus.

For this meeting, my ministry team has completed months of preparation. They have set up the latest state-of-the-art sound equipment. They use laser-guided and computer-driven technologies to relay my voice to the far horizon. I am able to whisper into the microphone and be heard as if I am face to face with each person in that mass of humanity before us. What will you say if I hand you the microphone? What will you say?

I start to preach. I tell the people God loves them and has given His only Son to die so that they can enter eternal life with Him. I ask them to accept Jesus as their Savior. Are you ready for this? – *1,093,000 lost souls respond*!

This actually happened in our Millennium Crusade in Lagos, Nigeria. On that night 1,093,000 people repeated the sinner's prayer. Then they filled out registration cards saying that they had accepted Christ and wanted follow-up ministry. At the end of that six-day event we counted a total of 3,450,000 people who had registered decisions for Jesus! *Can you say, Hallelujah*?!

I have been an evangelist since 1975, preaching face to face with maybe 100 million people over that span of time. But, in just the past three and one half years, I have seen more than 34 million souls come to the Lord. I've never seen crowds so hungry for God like this. Never.

Even though I have a great organization that has worked with me for thirty years to see this harvest, we are amazed at what is taking place. I want to convince you that if you are a follower of Jesus, this same thing can happen to you – even without an organization like mine.

Please, stand next to me. You may not believe it yet, but you belong at my side on this platform.

The truth is that while you and I may be human beings, as children of God we are much more than that. We are agents of omnipotence. This means that unlimited power is at our fingertips. It also means that there are no great men working in God's Kingdom. Rather, there is a great God at work in human beings who have childlike faith. You have not yet seen what God wants to do through you. This is what I hope you will come to believe with all your heart by the time you finish reading the stories in this book.

You may be a housewife, a grocery clerk, a policeman, a teacher, a student, a secretary, a delivery person, a hamburger flipper, a pastor, an executive – look in the mirror. If you belong to Jesus, God is preparing a platform for you. He will gather your crowd, great or small, from one lost soul to a desperate crowd of millions. It doesn't matter. The message is the same. You know it as well as I do.

In His Word the Lord tells us that it is His great pleasure to use the simple to confound the wise, the weak to confound the strong, people of no great credentials to speak His truth to kings and presidents and to vast crowds of people desperate to hear the Gospel. You have no place to hide from His call. Do not take this lightly. If you have managed to read this far, then I believe this book is a divine appointment for you.

I am Reinhard Bonnke. Everything that I do you can do ten times over. I want to help you prepare yourself for the days of harvest ahead. Come close to me and let me tell you stories that will convince you that what I say is true.

You can do this.

&

CHAPTER ONE

BLESSED OUT OF HER SHOES

She stood weeping at the far edge of the crowd, beyond my field of vision. Two hundred thousand gathered in Uhuru Park that day. I preached, and we saw thousands come to the Lord. Healings manifested among the people. I was thrilled with another day of obeying the Lord and seeing His power to save sinners. But Teresia Wairimu was not a sinner, and she did not come forward. I never knew she was there.

She had soaked her pillow for countless days before I came to her city of Nairobi in 1988. In recent months, her dream of serving God through serving her family had been shattered. The grief of this loss tore at her soul like a raging windstorm.

From childhood, Teresia had longed to serve the Lord. Attending church had filled her imagination with wonderful desires to marry a minister. When she finally came of age she met a charming European missionary. With this man, everything fell into place in her mind. The desire to serve God and the desire to serve this missionary merged into one. She could see no negatives.

Her parents did not approve. To them, a racially mixed union was a recipe for disaster. Besides, they were a respected business family, and were ashamed to think that their daughter would marry outside traditional African values. But in the thrall of love, and in her intense desire to serve the Lord, Teresia felt sure that God had provided the answer to her prayers in this wonderful

Christian man. She became willing to go against her parents' wishes to marry him.

It was a decision that haunted her a dozen years later when her missionary husband turned against her. No amount of appealing to his Christian faith made any difference. He took cruel advantage of a male-dominated court system to divorce her, and leave her and their daughter with no support.

How this story touches my heart. Like Teresia, I knew the longing to serve God as a child. When I was just ten years old in Germany I heard the voice of the Lord calling me to Africa. I also knew the desire to be married to one who shared that calling. I cannot imagine where I would be today, or how I would carry out God's call, if my precious Anni had ever turned against me. The very thought of it produces enough pain in my heart to silence all of my sermons. I am deeply touched by Teresia's agony.

As she stood weeping in Uhuru Park that hot and steamy day, she could sense the great gulf between the two of us. It was more than physical. I preached with a confidence she could not know. She had been cruelly discarded by the one man she had most wanted to please. As she stood there, she blamed herself for choosing so badly in her desire for a ministry mate. She further blamed herself for not being able to make the marriage work in spite of her husband's problems. Perhaps her husband's problems were actually her fault, she thought. She had not been good enough, not enough like Jesus to change his heart. Round and round her thoughts spun like the arms of a ceaseless windmill, beating her down, down, down.

She had no place to go. Her family would now reject her. They would tell her that she had only gotten what she deserved. She couldn't bring herself to even tell them of the divorce. The church was no better. Divorce was a terrible shame among Kenyan Christians; the kiss of death to anyone with a desire for ministry.

The only refuge Teresia found was in God. Though she felt rejected, Teresia somehow knew in the core of her soul that God had not rejected her. She was cast aside by a bad husband, not abandoned by a good God. She clung to the hope that someday, somehow, somewhere, God would arise and give her feet a solid place to stand again. A place no devil of Hell could ever take from her.

This is why she wept as she stood at the far perimeter of the crowd in Uhuru Park. As she describes it, she heard my voice preaching the Word of God with positive power and authority. The very sound of this kind of preaching caused hope to leap up in her heart. She had not heard the Gospel preached that way. The ministers she had known had been trained in seminaries. They had been taught not to raise their audiences' hopes, lest someone be disappointed and blame God in their despair. Even the hope of the Good News had been watered down so that unbelievers might not be offended.

But the Reinhard Bonnke that she saw that day preached the uncompromised Gospel, and let the chips fall where they may. He shouted the Good News into his microphone with gusto. The way he spoke and the way he moved on the stage told everyone that here was a man who believed his message and would stake his life on it. He acted like he really knew the God he preached about.

If Reinhard Bonnke can be that way, Teresia thought, *then I can too.* And tears of longing and hope spilled from her eyes.

When I called for the sick to come forward, Teresia watched as I laid hands on them. Blind eyes opened, lame people began to walk, people who were deaf could suddenly repeat my whispers, word for word. It was like another page being written in the Book of Acts.

Teresia saw that I possessed a living "fire" that was beyond the cold religious embers of her own experience. This was the gift she sought with tears that day. She would settle for nothing less. From the very depths of her soul she cried out, "God, oh please God, if you can give Bonnke 100,000 souls, give me one hundred, just one hundred, Lord, and I'll be a happy woman."

Once Teresia said this, she knew something deep down in her heart; she knew that to receive her answer from God, Reinhard Bonnke would have to lay his hands on her head and pray for her.

What is this? I don't know. It is something I cannot explain except to say, she had faith like the woman who touched the fringe of Jesus' cloak. It was not Jesus' idea that the woman in the Bible do this thing. It was the woman's idea. In fact, Jesus was on His way to heal someone else when she chased Him down and touched the fringe of His cloak. When she did, she was healed. Jesus turned to her and said, "Daughter, your faith has made you well."

Teresia's faith was like this woman's faith. Somehow she knew that I must lay my hands on her and pray for her, then she could step into her full blessing from God.

This is not a formula for getting anything from God. I tell you there is no special power in my hands or my prayer, anymore than there was special virtue in the fringe of Jesus' robe.

It was the faith of the woman in the Bible that mattered. And it was Teresia's faith that gave this idea of my laying hands on her its peculiar power.

Teresia left Uhuru Park that day without a chance for prayer. The crowds were pressing around the platform with so many needs, and God was directing me to the ones He was healing. I never knew she was there.

Eight years passed before our paths crossed again. Teresia spent those years making a new life in Nairobi. She raised her daughter to young womanhood. She rose from the ashes of her shattered dreams to build new relationships with a small group of Christian women. They looked to her for spiritual guidance, and from time to time, she would minister among her friends. But her ministry lacked the power she had seen in Uhuru Park that day. Her spirit was still crushed by her failed marriage, and she knew she had not arrived at God's highest calling for her.

During those eight years Teresia also tracked my speaking schedule through the ministry magazine. She was always on the lookout for a city where I would be preaching to a smaller crowd. This would increase her chance of being prayed over.

It happened in Oslo, Norway in the spring of '96. She was excited to learn that I would be speaking there in a local church because she had friends in Oslo. Immediately she called them and made arrangements to stay with them. They agreed to bring her to the meeting.

She saved her money and bought a round trip ticket. All of her friends in Nairobi prayed with her as she left, believing that she would return with the fire of God's Spirit that she longed for.

Teresia was the first one through the doors of the church in Oslo when they opened. Her friends escorted her to the very front row. She waited there as the room continued to fill up. A local woman approached her.

"There is something that you need from God," the woman said, "and God spoke to me that He will give it to you."

This was wonderful confirmation. Teresia thanked her and replied, "That is good, but I am still waiting."

When I came to the platform as the service began, I knew immediately that Teresia was there. It is hard to miss an African lady in a Norwegian church. She stood out like an island of color in a sea of gray, dressed in her traditional African robes. I could see that she was trembling from the very start of the meeting.

Teresia had come with one thing in mind; when I gave the altar call for the sick, she would run forward for prayer. In her mind, she was sick. She felt sick with frustration and ineffectiveness in her ministry. This is how she justified in her own mind, coming for prayer at the call for the sick.

Her focus on this idea made it impossible for her to actually concentrate on my sermon. In fact, I preached a salvation message. That fact did not register with her. I challenged those who wanted to accept Jesus as Savior to stand up. She shot up like a lightning bolt. Then suddenly, she realized that this was not a call for the sick, and she sheepishly sat down again. She had waited eight long years; she would wait another twenty minutes for my next invitation.

When I finally announced that I would pray for the sick, she raced to the front and stood before me, trembling with anticipation.

She knew that she was within moments of receiving the answer to the prayer that she had prayed in Uhuru Park eight years before. She would receive the anointing to minister in power and authority, just the way Reinhard Bonnke ministered.

I will never forget what happened next. Nor will Teresia ever remember. To this day she does not know that I actually laid my hands on her. She has no memory of that. The fire of God had nothing to do with the touch of my hands, but I did place them on her head. Only for an instant, because she was ripped from beneath my hands by a mighty force that threw her twenty yards through the air and landed her on her back near the front row of seats from which she had come. The force of this action was so strong that both of her shoes flew from her feet. One shoe, I can still see it, sailed end over end far out into the middle of that gray Norwegian audience. It has never been seen again. Who knows, someone might have taken it as a souvenir.

I moved on to pray for the others. Much later, Teresia recalls rousing from an unconscious state and hearing my voice saying, "Miracles are happening, miracles are happening." That's all she remembers.

The miracles of God are always a sign and a wonder. We are left to shake our heads and say, "Praise God, praise God, praise God." The great miracle that happened that night in Oslo is still happening to this day in Nairobi, Kenya. Teresia Wairimu is on fire.

The Oslo meeting closed. I left to return to Germany. Teresia could not get up from the floor of that church. As she regained consciousness, her body would not properly respond to the commands from her brain. Her legs were so wobbly that her friends had to carry her from the church to the car. They drove her home, then carried her from the car into the house and deposited her on the bed in the guest bedroom. That's when they gave her back the one remaining shoe of the pair she had worn that night. It is a shoe she has kept to remind herself of what God did for her that night. She knew in her heart that she would never be the same.

The story might end here. It has ended here for many. They receive a great visitation of God's Spirit, then they do nothing to work it out in their life. But God had not anointed Teresia for nothing. She had not received her blessing for nothing. She had come for the power to minister, and minister she would.

Upon arrival back in Nairobi she called her girl-friends to a Friday prayer meeting at her house. They came. Seventeen of them. She preached with a power she had never known before. When she asked for the sick to come forward, she did not offer a weak religious prayer. She did not ask for God to please heal someone if it was in His great divine will to do so. No, she commanded the sick to be healed in Jesus' name, and healings began to manifest.

The next Friday there were 55 women at her house. The next Friday, 105, and the next, 200 women showed up. She and her circle of girl-friends began to look for a school building in which to meet. By now some of the notable and documented healings from her ministry were being talked about around the city. They found a city auditorium that held 2000, but 4000 women showed up. They had to open all the doors and windows to try to accommodate the overflow. She moved to the Jomo Kenyatta Convention Center, which held 5,000. Twelve thousand came.

At this point some pastors in the city began to denounce her and tell their people not to attend her meetings because she was a divorced woman. The people ignored them. Some came out of curiosity, others out of need. But when they arrived at a Teresia Wairimu meeting, they did not hear about a woman's divorce, they heard the Gospel of Jesus Christ. They saw cancers healed, AIDS healed, blind eyes opened, and deaf ears unstopped.

Finally, Teresia went to the city council and asked to have the use of Uhuru Park, where Bonnke had preached in 1988. They made a contract with her, giving her use of the park for the first Sunday of every month. Her crowds swelled, and now included men as well as women.

The weeping woman in Uhuru Park in 1988 had desperately prayed, "God, oh please God, if you can give Bonnke 100,000 souls, give me one hundred, just one hundred, Lord, and I'll be a happy woman." Teresia Wairimu is today a very happy woman. Her name is a household word in Africa. The ministers who once preached against her have apologized and begged her forgiveness.

When I heard of her breakthrough I went to the Lord in prayer. "Why Lord," I asked, "did you choose a divorced woman for this great ministry? We have so many wonderful men in our Bible Schools, men who pursue You with all of their hearts. Why did You choose Teresia and not one of them?"

His answer affected me deeply. He said, "I chose Teresia because I wanted to show the world that I could take a broken vessel and make a vessel of honor."

How this humbled me. We are not chosen for our great qualities. We are flawed servants who must depend totally on Him. I have enjoyed the benefits of a strong marriage to my Anni all these years. But this great happiness is not the secret of my success. Teresia suffered the ultimate humiliation of divorce, but God lifted her to a platform of powerful ministry. All to the glory of God.

Two years after Oslo, in 1998, exactly ten years after I had first preached in Uhuru Park, I visited Nairobi with my wife Anni. We stayed in a hotel that borders the park. I made sure that we would arrive there on the first Sunday of the month.

I stood at the far edge of the crowd, beyond her field of vision. Two hundred thousand gathered in Uhuru Park that day. Teresia preached with power and authority and saw thousands come to the Lord. Healings manifested. It was as if another page was written in the Book of Acts. She was doubtless thrilled with another day of obeying the Lord, and seeing His power to save sinners. But I was not a sinner, and I did not come forward. She never knew I was there, smiling from ear to ear.

✑

Why do we make so much of a person's qualifications for ministry? When I am weak then I am strong said the Apostle Paul. We are qualified by God's omnipotence, not by our pitiful strengths.

CHAPTER TWO

QUASIMODO'S DREAM

She never missed church, but it was nerve wracking to get her there. First her wheelchair had to be moved near the car. Then she had to be helped out of the chair and carefully positioned to get inside. Her crooked and stiffened spine made it impossible for her to bend at the proper angle. She would receive a cruel jolt as she dropped onto the seat. Then, her legs would have to be placed inside the car. Her hips had been permanently dislodged from their sockets, and moving her legs would cause her to scream in pain.

Her husband would beg her to stay at home. So would her friends who sometimes took her to church. Tears of pain would roll from her eyes, but her jaw remained firm. She would not be denied another opportunity to be in the house of the Lord. "Take Quasimodo to church," Jean Neil would say, gritting her teeth, with a fierce little twinkle in her eye.

During each meeting Jean would be able to sit on a thick cushion for only a few minutes. Then the pain would become unbearable, and she would pull herself up on her crutches and stagger to the wall. There, she would lean against it to relieve the searing pain between her lower back and her hips. She would stand that way, draped across her crutches, for the better part of an hour. No one could attend that church and not be constantly reminded that Jean Neil was in terrible pain.

For this reason many prayers were made for her healing. The pastor prayed, the youth group prayed, the women's group prayed. Every congregational prayer time included a request for Jean's healing. Always her friends searched for answers. "Was something wrong with their prayers? Why wouldn't God heal such a faithful servant as this?" Jean never lost hope, but her faith was sent through many ups and downs over the years.

Her basic problem was a bad back. Jean had known this from her youth. But she had never let it stop her from a rough-and-tumble approach to life. She was athletic and mischievous, a prankster, an instigator. She was the kind to do things on a dare.

Those friends who knew her best, appreciated her spunk. They knew that she had been raised for fifteen years in a terrible home for girls in Jersey. She had been beaten with stinging nettles for wetting the bed as a toddler. She had been tortured in ice baths for speaking out of turn to her caregivers. She had been fed water and stale bread. She had been stripped naked and beaten in front of the other girls for making wisecracks. But they could never beat the wisecracking out of Jean. She never lost her knack for a quick remark. She had developed a strong and defiant will to thrive in the face of great odds. It was her gift.

She had married John Neil, and they had made their life together in Rugby, England. Jean had become a Christian but John had not. Still, things were going well for them when suddenly she had taken a bad fall. It had ruptured her tailbone and this had accelerated the deterioration of her spine. A series of operations, some of which had gone badly, had fused several disks. After her last operation she was placed in a plaster cast for six months.

Emerging from the cast, she was told that she would never walk again. On top of that, her heart and lungs had become weakened through the prolonged pain, as well as the many pain medications. Specially formulated pills were necessary to keep her heart pumping. She had also become dependent on inhalers and oxygen. One top British surgeon gave her a fifty-fifty chance of improvement with a final risky operation to reconstruct her backbone. Every day that she lived, Jean weighed her pain against the risk of that final desperate operation.

Meanwhile, she kept going to church. In spite of her condition she took an active role as a youth leader. She had a heart for the teenagers and invested herself in them. They appreciated her for it, and were inspired by her example, knowing how much she endured just to be with them.

Then something happened that would change her life forever. A three-year-old toddler at church, a little boy, walked up to Jean and asked to pray for her. She took his little hands in hers and let him pray his simple, childlike prayer. He asked that God would heal her. Something began stirring, deep in Jean's soul.

That night she had two distinct and vivid dreams. In the first dream she underwent the spinal surgery, and she died on the operating table. She watched the doctor tell her husband that her heart simply had become too weakened to endure the process. She awoke with a start. There could be no mistake about the meaning of this dream – if she chose to go with the surgery, death was coming for her. She wondered, *could it have been a dream from my own anxieties?* She went back to sleep.

This time Jean had another very different dream. She was in a large cavernous room with twelve other people in wheelchairs. She heard the voice of a man speaking. It was a distinctive voice with a foreign accent. She saw the man emerge in front of the wheelchairs. He went to the first chair and prayed for a woman. He commanded her to get up. She got up, but then sat back down in utter defeat. Then the man came to Jean's chair. He prayed for her, and she took off running from her wheelchair, totally healed.

The next day Jean visited her pastor. She was frightened. She told him she feared the end of her life was near. Her pastor suggested that she did not focus on the first dream but the second. He said that a whole new life could be near for her – a life of health and wholeness. She had to choose which dream to believe, the dream of death or the dream of life?

Jean rejected her fears and chose life. She began to describe the second dream to her friends and family. She could even describe the physical description of the man who had prayed for her, and the description of the room they were in, and the sound of his voice. She began to look forward to whatever, or whomever, this agent of God's power might be.

Two weeks later a youth convention was to be held in the National Exhibition Center in Birmingham, England. The little youth group from Rugby would, of course, attend. Jean Neil would go with them. She heard that the speaker would be Reinhard Bonnke. His reputation as an evangelist included many stories of miraculous healings. This event took place in 1988.

She had her husband, John prepare a special ambulance for her to ride in. Since he worked for an ambulance company, this was something he could do. She told her friends that she believed that if Reinhard Bonnke prayed for her she would begin to improve. At this point she could not bring herself to say definitely that I was the man she had seen in her dream. Her faith for healing was not yet complete.

I arrived in Birmingham and stayed at the home of a friend there. The morning of the meeting I felt a strong urge to pray. As I prayed, I sensed the presence of the Holy Spirit with me in an unusual way. I began to ask, "Lord, what do you want to do today? What miracle will you perform in this meeting?"

I entered the Convention Center hall through a stage door. There was a thick curtain that I was told to go through, and then I would be on the platform. As I pushed through the curtain, there was a young man standing there on crutches. I didn't see him in time, and I brushed him as I passed. He fell straight onto his back. The people attending me quickly saw to him, and pushed me onto the stage. I was told later, as the service got under way, that the young man was not knocked down by me, but by the power of God. He got up and did not need his crutches anymore.

The cavernous room was filled with nearly 12,000 youth delegates and their adult supervisors. I sat on my chair and waited to be announced. As I did I looked across the crowd and continued in deep conversation with the Lord. "Lord what are you doing here tonight?"

As my gaze fell across the wheelchairs, the Lord directed my attention to one lady at the far left. I sensed the Spirit saying to me, "*That woman in that wheelchair will be healed today.*"

From her wheelchair Jean watched me on the stage. She thought that I certainly bore a strong resemblance to the man in her dream. She looked around the hall at the other wheelchairs. She didn't count them, but there were perhaps twelve others in her condition. When I got up to preach Jean knew my voice from her dream. The tone and the accent seemed identical. She began to feel a powerful sense of anticipation.

I was on fire with the Spirit. I preached a salvation message to those young people. When I gave an altar call, nearly 1,500 of them responded. I was ecstatic. It was a glorious day. Then suddenly, the host of the meeting came to me on the platform and said, "Reinhard, I have hired this room only until six o'clock. We have to clear the room."

I looked at my watch and saw that we only had fifteen minutes before the room must be cleared. I was stricken. *Oh, no*, I thought, *I have not prayed for the sick.*

Without any delay I hurried down from the platform and went to the first wheelchair I saw in front of me. A lady sat there. I said, "I want to pray for you."

I placed my hands on her. I could feel the power of the Spirit like electricity in my hands. I prayed, then said, "Stand up in Jesus' name."

She stood, but she was very shaky. On her face was an expression of irritation, as if I had no right to do this to her. She sat back down. I knew she was not healed. *Oh, no*, I thought, *this is not the woman God showed me.*

At this point, someone in the room had a video camera running. What follows was recorded and has been viewed again and again by many audiences in the years since this meeting.

I switched gears. I remembered that the woman God had shown me was to the left. I hopped up, and looked to the left until I saw her. Then I raced all the way across the room, the camera following me. I was sprinting against the clock to get to her before they cleared that hall.

Jean Neil was sitting in that wheelchair. Her husband John stood behind her, gripping the handles of the chair. I had never seen them before. I knew nothing about their circumstances nor what had brought them here. I glanced at John, and he looked at me with a look as cold as stone. I knelt down in front of Jean, and said, "I've come to pray for you. *You're going to be healed today.*"

I will never forget her reply, "I know, I know, I know!" she cried.

What Jean knew was that her second dream was coming true before her very eyes. Her faith reached out.

I said, "OK, I will pray for you, and you will stand up."

John said, "What do you mean, stand up? My wife has no hips. Her hips are not attached."

I said, "All I know is all things are possible with God. I will pray for you, and you will stand up."

I laid my hands on her and I prayed. Then I commanded her to stand up. Slowly, with great determination, she stood up, and then she sort of slumped forward onto the floor. I thought, oh, no, Lord what have I done?

But then I realized she had not collapsed back into her wheelchair, she had fallen forward. This was in the right direction at least. Then suddenly I knew that she had not fallen because her hips could not carry her, she had fallen under the power of God. She was slain in the Spirit, the same thing that happened to the young man on crutches as I brushed him on the stage.

I quickly bent down over her. I said, "Jesus is healing you."

"I know, I know," she said. Then she looked at me and said, "I feel as if I am under anesthetic."

"Doctor Jesus is operating on you," I cried.

At this point, as Jean tells it, she felt powerful, incredible things happening inside her body. She felt as if she was placed on a stretcher and her body was being pulled straight. She felt her hips go into their sockets. One of her legs was two inches shorter than the other. It grew out to be the same length as the other. Then, she said it was as if a hot rod of steel went down the full length of her spine. Her bones, tissues and muscles, which had atrophied, began to flex and pulse with new life.

I said to her, "Get up, in Jesus' name."

I looked at John. I thought he would punch me. He said, "What if she falls?"

I said, "I'll be here. I'll be here. Now, get up."

Slowly Jean began to gather herself from the floor. She stood to her feet.

"Now, walk in Jesus' name."

The video camera was rolling. People were standing on chairs all around us. We were totally surrounded by onlookers. Jean had on a red hat, a beret. Everyone in the room saw that beret fly upward as she suddenly disappeared from under it. To me it seemed as if she made a sudden leap like a grasshopper makes at the moment you least expect it. Before I could tell what happened that woman was gone.

Jean Neil raced around that building, hands in the air, praising God, crying with joy. Her second dream had just happened. Not death, but a brand new life.

She said her legs were not in the least bit wobbly. They were pumping with strength and incredible power. I kept calling into the microphone, "Where is that woman? Where is that woman?"

The people kept answering. "Over there, over there, over there." And each time they were pointing to a different place.

I was still looking for her in the direction she had gone when suddenly she was right behind me. She had gone completely around that building.

The place was bedlam. So much crying. So much praising God. So many tears of joy.

I asked Jean if she would go up onto the stage so that the people could learn what had just happened. She whirled and bounded up the steps to the platform. They were quite steep. It was a testimony in itself. She was completely restored. John followed, in shock, bringing along the wheelchair. I followed.

On stage Jean was dancing around with her hands in the air like a boxer who had just won the heavyweight title. The crowd was cheering. Jean was waving. I asked her whom she was waving to, and she said to her pastor and friends from her church in Rugby. Then I learned for the first time the extent of her illnesses. It is good that I did not know beforehand. It might have affected my thoughts and my faith to pray for her. I don't know, God knows, and God is good.

"Give us a demonstration," I said.

"Of what?" Jean retorted, in her wonderful, sarcastic way.

"Do something you could not do before," I explained.

"Oh," she said, as if she did not know what I had meant.

Then she began to bend down and touch her toes, do deep knee bends, run in place. She went through a regular workout for the people. They cheered and applauded and praised God, until somebody remembered that we had to clear the hall.

I don't know who paid the bill for the extra time. I was just the guest speaker, and it was time for me to go back to Germany. I said goodbye to the people.

Only after arriving back home did I learn the full extent of this miracle. My phone began to ring. People were hearing about this miracle in countries around the world. Because I know human nature, I know that sometimes those who sit in wheelchairs are not crippled. In Jean Neil's case, the many people from her church who knew her were confirming the power of this testimony. Soon her doctors added their confirmation to the story. The news media went into a frenzy over it. It was a healing that shook many in the church from their lethargy concerning the power of God to heal.

When I left town, Jean Neil was beginning a brand new life. She went home to Rugby and raced up the stairs into her house. Her daughter was in the sitting room with her boyfriend. When she heard feet running up the stairs she thought it was a burglar.

"Go see to it," she urged her boyfriend.

He was a bit frightened. "Maybe it's your mother," he suggested, hopefully.

"My mother's a crippled old woman," she said. "She can't run up the stairs."

Having opened the door, Jean heard this remark. For the first time in her life she realized what her family thought of her. Quasimodo was more than a bittersweet joke. To her loved ones, it had been a hard reality.

She walked into the room with her daughter. "When Jesus heals you, you can run up stairs," she said.

"Mother!" Her daughter burst into tears. Jean ran up and down the stairs for her. Then they embraced and cried and cried and cried some more.

Eventually John parked the ambulance. He came up the stairs to join them, carrying the wheelchair.

Jean says that when she awoke the next morning she was paralyzed with a sudden fear and could not move. "John," she said, in a trembling voice.

He sat up quickly. "Yes, dear. What is it?"

For a moment she could not speak. "Was it just a dream, John? Did I have another dream?"

"No, it was not a dream, darling. It really happened. I was there."

She leaped from the bed, dancing around the room. "I will fix breakfast. I will do the dishes. I will clean the house. I will go to the store." And with that she left him still wiping the sleep from his eyes.

It was Sunday, the day to go to church. After breakfast, Jean put on her cloak and headed out the door. No one would take her to church on this day. She would walk.

She hurried down the front steps and across the street. She took huge breaths of fresh air, needing no more inhaler, no more oxygen, no more drugs. Her heart was singing and overflowing with gratitude.

Then she heard a rattling sound behind her. She stopped and turned. There was John, hurrying after her with the wheelchair.

"What are you doing, John?"

He stopped. "What if you fall?" He stood there with a helpless look on his face. He was still her protector, and he still had trouble believing she had been healed, even though he had been there to see it.

"Take it back home, John. You're embarrassing me. I will never sit in that chair again."

He did. And she never did. Even when a TV documentary crew offered her £1,000 just to make a picture in the chair, she refused.

Her story was a sensation in Europe. A couple months later another evangelist asked Jean to give her testimony at one of his meetings in England. Many sick people were present. When she finished telling her story she sat down. The evangelist asked her why she was sitting down.

"I'm finished," she said.

"No," he replied, "you have not even begun, Jean Neil. Stand up. It's time for you to pray for the sick."

"But I've never prayed for the sick. Please don't make me do this, please."

He called the sick people in the audience to the front. He told them that Jean Neil would now pray for them. They had been inspired by her story. Reaching out with a new level of faith, they came forward.

Jean took the evangelist to one side on the platform. "Please, you pray first and I'll watch you. I'll learn by watching you."

"Praying for the sick is an anointing," he replied. "You don't need practice. Now go pray for them. God is going to show you big things, Jean Neil."

Jean turned around and walked to the first person in line. She found herself looking at his mid-thigh. Jean is a bit shorter than the average. She bent her head back, looking up at him, and said, "How tall are you?"

She heard his voice as if from the clouds, "Seven feet."

She laughed aloud. Then she turned around and walked back to the evangelist.

"You said God would show me *big* things. Does He have a sense of humor? Take a look at this guy."

The evangelist, who was praying for others, was not amused. "Ask him what is wrong with him, and then lay hands on him and pray."

Jean was just a housewife who had been given a new body a few weeks before. She had no idea that it would require her to become an agent of omnipotence. She wasn't quite sure yet that she wanted to be one. But it seemed to go with the territory.

She returned to the seven-foot-tall young man and looked up at him. "What is wrong with you?"

"My shoulders are frozen," he said. "I am scheduled for surgery on Monday, to try to get some movement back."

Jean nodded. Then she pondered what to do. With sudden inspiration she went to the front row and took an empty chair. Bringing it back with her she placed it down in front of the young man. Then she proceeded to climb up on it.

The evangelist saw her and threw up his hands. He hurried over to her. "What on earth are you doing?"

"His shoulders are frozen. I can't reach them."

"You couldn't reach his shoulders even if you stand on the back of that chair. For Heaven's sake, get down. You don't have to lay hands on his shoulders to pray for him. Just take his hands and pray."

"Oh," Jean replied.

She got down from the chair and put it aside. Giving a big sigh, she took the young man by the hands and prayed a simple prayer for healing. Suddenly, the full seven-foot frame of the young man fell like a tall tree straight over onto his back – kerthunk! There was no one to catch his fall.

Jean was horrified. She understood the physical potential of such a fall. He might have suffered a concussion, a spinal injury, or worse.

She ran over to the evangelist. "He fell straight back and hit the floor," she said. "If God healed his shoulders then I'm afraid He's now broken his back. This is terrible."

"That is not terrible. It is the power of God on him. He will be just fine," the evangelist said, and went on with his praying.

Jean did not believe it. She hurried back to the prone form of the young man and bent down near his head. "I'm so sorry, young man. Are you alright? Are you?"

For a few moments the young man could not reply. He seemed only semi-conscious. Then he roused himself. Jean helped him to his feet. He stood to his full height and began to exercise his arms, raising them high over his head, doing things he had not been able to do before, one experiment after another. Soon he was shouting and praising God for his healing.

It so happened that his wife was in a wheelchair across the room. Seeing her husband's release from bondage she leaped from her chair totally healed. She ran over to join him in his celebration.

Jean Neil stood watching, wide-eyed. God was indeed showing her *big* things.

That night Jean was launched into a ministry that continues to this day. Her husband, John has come to know Jesus as his Savior. Her entire family serves the Lord today. They travel the world telling the story of her healing. The video that was shot that day has been shown again and again to audiences around the world, inspiring faith in sick people. Scores of remarkable miracles are recorded as Jean prays for the sick. She preaches the Gospel to her audiences and thousands come to know Jesus as their Savior.

But I cannot leave Jean's story without sharing one more incident that reveals so much: Jean never said no to an invitation to share her testimony. The phone would ring, she would answer, someone would ask her to testify, she would check her calendar, say yes, and the meeting was on. This was simply her new way of life.

One day the phone rang, and she was invited to speak at a small church in Jersey. She accepted without thinking. Putting the phone down, she suddenly had misgivings. Unpleasant feelings about Jersey welled up within her, feelings from her childhood. She had never wanted to go back to Jersey, but, she told herself, this was no pleasure tour. She decided that she would go back to share about the new Jean Neil, and she would simply ignore the past.

At the end of the service the people came forward for prayer as they usually did. Finally, after finishing her time of prayer for the sick, two older women approached her. As they stood before her one of them said, "Jean, do you think you could find it in your heart to forgive us?"

"Forgive you," Jean said. "I don't even know you."

"Yes, you do," said the lady. "We were your caregivers at the school."

A part of Jean Neil that had been deeply buried suddenly sprang to life. The beatings with the stinging nettles. The ice bath tortures. The diet of bread and water. The cold nights lying naked beneath one thin sheet. The humiliations in front of the other girls. All of these painful memories came rushing back.

Without a thought, and before she could stop herself, Jean took both of these women by the throat, one in each hand. "How can I forgive you?" she rasped. In her rage she felt that she would literally beat them both on the spot.

In that moment, the voice of the Spirit spoke clearly and sharply inside of her. *"If you do not forgive them, Jean, I will not forgive you."*

She trembled in her rage and in her long buried desire for vengeance. *"But you didn't go through what I went through,"* she protested internally.

"I went through much more."

She suddenly knew that it was true. Her suffering could never equal His. That is when Jean Neil discovered that in her heart she could not embrace vengeance. She belonged to Him. She let it go, and she released the two women. "I am so sorry," she said. "I must forgive you. No, I do forgive you. Jesus makes all things new."

The pent-up dam of feelings broke for the three of them. With great weeping they embraced and let Jesus bury the pain and shame of the past, as only Jesus can.

Over the years since 1988, I gradually came to learn the details of Jean's story that I have shared with you here. It was years later that she told me of the dream. It just fascinates me the way God worked in two different lives to bring this miracle about. She even heard my accent in her dream. Such detail! And she had never heard me preach before. She only knew me by vague reputation.

After that morning of prayer, God pointed Jean out to me in the crowd of 12,000 at the National Exhibition Center and told me He would heal her. In my haste to pray for the sick, anyone who was sick, I thought that I had made a bad mistake in praying for the wrong woman. But God had anticipated that very action.

For Jean it was the final detail from her dream that confirmed in her mind that she was seeing the actual fulfillment of that second dream. Her healing was imminent. Now, her faith was in full force. She was so ready when I came to her and said, "Jesus is going to heal you."

"I know, I know, I know," she cried. I can still hear the marvelous anticipation in her voice.

What a mighty God we serve!

❧

I know people who would rather do nothing than do something wrong in serving the Lord. They have put pride above God's own heart. When I prayed for the wrong woman, God had shown that very detail in Jean Neil's dream. If I had not made the so-called mistake, her faith might never have been inspired to reach its miraculous destination.

CHAPTER THREE

A BOY IN THE HEADLIGHTS

I switched off the generator. The gasoline powered Briggs-and-Stratton engine sputtered and fell silent. The lights strung between poles around the green canvas tent winked out. I was plunged into darkness.

It was 1977. Another African crusade had come to an end. The singing of a million crickets seemed to fill the night around me, reminding me of where I stood. I was in a large open field in the northern Transvaal Basin of South Africa. I had pitched our tent where the rolling grasslands bear the occasional thorn tree. The songs of crickets and grasshoppers ruled the summer night, along with the croaking of frogs seeking an insect feast.

After my preaching and praying for the sick, the African crowd of several thousand had slowly wandered away to their mud-and-thatch huts. They had gone in every direction of the compass. As members of various tribes, these people lived in scattered villages surrounded by kraals, enclosures made of rough pickets.

Meanwhile, the local pastor had driven his wife home in their car. They lived in a modest western-style house a few miles away, and had provided a guest bedroom for me. I had remained behind to shut down the lights at the tent. On this final night, I wanted to spend some time alone with God before I followed.

I looked up. There were no stars in the sky. Not the faintest glow penetrated the clouds. I looked right and left into nothing but blackness. Moving my hand in front of my face, I could detect no movement. It still amazed me to be reminded of how dark a night can be in primitive Africa. Electricity is a rare treasure.

How I loved this moment alone in the wild. I drank it up, inhaling the fresh air, feeling a cooling breeze on my face. The Lord was standing with me. He had brought me to this place. I had come in response to a dream that had invaded my sleep for many nights, forever changing my ministry. Night after night, I had seen a map of Africa washed in the blood of Jesus Christ. Each time I had seen it, the Holy Spirit had whispered the words in my heart, *Africa shall be saved.*

The dream had finally become a waking vision that stood before my eyes, prompting me to leave my small mission station in Lesotho and move to Johannesburg. I had stepped out by faith to establish a new evangelistic organization called Christ for all Nations. A handful of partners had helped me buy this modest tent, which at once, had proven too small. I was preaching to crowds that stood around it, unable to squeeze into the sheltered area. It mattered not. They listened to my voice amplified through loudspeakers set on light poles outside.

As we had taken our crusade into tribal lands, we had discovered that my name, "Bonnke," was a Zulu word meaning "everyone together." What a happy coincidence! Surely a Bonnke crusade brought these people together in record numbers, even if some came expecting to see a Zulu preacher. Hundreds were responding to the Gospel. What a privilege it was to follow and obey the vision from God. I thanked Him for so honoring me.

"Africa shall be saved," I whispered into the darkness, "Africa shall be saved."

Putting out my hands in case I miscalculated the direction, I slowly turned and walked toward the place where I had remembered parking my car. At last, I could detect its faint outline. I reached for the door handle and opened it, flooding the immediate area with light again. I got in and started the engine, switching on the headlights. Then I drove across the open field toward the place where a dirt lane would guide me to the pastor's house. I had traveled this route each night for the past week. I followed my tire tracks through the tall grass.

As I neared the edge of the field, suddenly a slight boy, just a teenager, ran into my path. He waved his arms to flag me down. I stopped and rolled down my window.

"Is something wrong?" I asked.

He would not come close to the window. I could see that he wanted to be polite. It was part of his tribal heritage.

"Please, Moruti Bonnke," he said, using the title of respect reserved for pastors, "I want you to lay hands on me and pray for me."

A great weariness was on me. I had finished a vigorous sermon under a strong anointing. Many had come to the Lord. I had prayed for the sick. The natural physical letdown that follows such effort had set in.

"How old are you, son?"

"Seventeen," he said.

"Why do you want me to pray for you?"

"I got saved in your crusade. Jesus has forgiven me of all my sins. But I knew you would pass here, and I wanted to ask you to pray that I would receive the Holy Spirit before I return to my village. It is far away."

This request went to the heart of my call to Africa. My weariness lifted at once.

"I will pray for you," I said, and got out of the car. I left the car running with the headlights on so that I could see what I was doing.

"What is your name, son?" I asked.

"David."

"I will pray for you, David." Then I began, "Lord, according to the promise of Your Word, I ask that You fill David with Your Holy Spirit." I laid my hands on his head. "Receive the gift of the Holy Spirit, in Jesus' name."

He undulated like a bolt of lightning had run down his spine. Then he began to cry and praise God. This was a familiar sight to my eyes. I had prayed for many people in the course of many meetings who had reacted in exactly the same way. I seldom understood what God had accomplished. I just had to leave it in God's hands and move on, trusting that the power of God would bear fruit in His own time.

After a few moments, I said good-bye to David, and wished him a safe walk back to his village. I climbed into my car and drove on toward my sleeping quarters. As my headlights panned away from him, David's slight barefoot form was swallowed up in that ink black night. I never expected to see him again. He was one of many I had prayed for in the past week, and God alone knew each of their paths. As I followed my tire tracks in the grass, I felt wearier than ever, my body craving sleep.

Months later in Johannesburg, I began to hear reports of a revival that had broken out in the tribal region of the Transvaal Basin. When I asked who the preacher was, I was told that he was no preacher at all. Just a boy whom God was using greatly. It never entered my mind that David was that boy. I had no idea.

A year later, I had launched a new evangelistic tool, sponsored by Christ for all Nations. It was a mighty tent, a modern marvel that could squeeze 10,000 people under one yellow canvas. Already, crowds were overflowing the new tent. Sometimes, more stood outside than inside. I had begun talking with designers about plans to build the world's largest transportable structure, a gigantic Gospel tent that would some day shelter 34,000 souls at one time. The vision of a blood-washed Africa was moving me toward larger and larger venues.

Meanwhile, with the new yellow tent, I returned for another week of meetings in the northern tribal region of South Africa. It was my intention to focus crusades in this area until I had saturated it with the Gospel. Along with the bigger tent, I had brought along an air-conditioned travel-trailer. I parked it beside the tent. That is where I stayed during the meetings.

One night after preaching I heard a knock at my door. I opened it, and there stood David. His face was beaming with joy.

"Moruti Bonnke," he said, "it is me, David."

"I remember you," I said, "I prayed for you to receive the Holy Spirit in the field that night."

"Yes. May I come in and tell you what has happened?"

"Of course. Please, do come in."

He came in, and I invited him to sit down. My wife, Anni, was with me. She made some hot tea, and we began to talk. "Tell me, David. What happened after I prayed for you?"

"Well," he said, "it was very far to my village that night. After you prayed, I walked home. It was like walking on air. I did not feel the journey. It was not until dawn that I arrived. As I first saw my village in the morning light, I noticed a woman leaving the kraal. She was carrying a bundle in her arms, and I thought that I could hear her crying. I knew this woman. She was well known in the village. The week before I came to the Christ for all Nations meeting, she had lost a child to black fever. I called to her, 'Mother, where are you going?'"

In South African tribal culture, "Mother" is a title of respect for any woman who has borne children. This is especially true if the person addressing her is a boy like David, not yet a man.

"She did not reply," David said, "but she came to me. She knew me. She was not weeping as I had thought, but she held out the bundle in her arms, and I could see that she carried her second child, a young boy. He was taken by a violent fever, and was making a very strange cry. This is the cry that I had heard. I could see that this child, too, soon would die. The woman would lose both of her children to the fever.

"Just hours ago, Moruti Bonnke, you had prayed that I would receive the Holy Spirit. I could still feel Him within me. When I saw this woman I felt love come from me like I had never known, I could not contain it. The Jesus that you preached about surely cared for this child, and this woman.

"It was against tribal rules," David said, "but I felt so much love that I decided to risk it. I asked her if I could pray for the sick child the way you had prayed for sick people in the tent meeting. I said, 'Mother, can I pray for your child?'

"She said, 'Yes, yes, anything, please.'

"I laid my hands on the child, and I could feel the fire of the fever burning in his head. I asked God to take the fever from the child. Suddenly, he stopped crying. The child sat up and said, 'Mommy, I'm hungry. I'm thirsty.' The mother was amazed. She felt the child's head and the fever was gone.

"That woman's eyes grew so large! She ran with the child to the village ahead of me. She went straight to the chief's house. She told him, 'David prayed for my child and healed him. Look, the fever is gone.' She fed the child and gave him water, and he seemed to recover his strength immediately. He went outside and began to play with the other children.

"I went to my hut. I began telling my family about your prayer for me, and about what had happened that morning. Suddenly, a runner came. He summoned me to an audience with the chief.

"I was afraid because the chief was so high above my family. I had never been to his house. He is our respected king, our royal leader. He is rich enough to support many wives and children. I came and bowed to him. The woman whose son had been healed was there with the boy.

"The chief said to me, 'David, I heard what you did for this mother. I have a daughter that no doctor can help. She is crippled. She was born with twisted limbs.' He said, 'I have taken her to the finest doctors in Cape Town, and they can do nothing. I have taken her to the witch doctors. Nothing has been able to help. Please go to her hut and pray for her as you prayed for this child today.'

"I told him that I would do as he commanded.

"The woman, whose child had been healed, went with me. When we entered the hut, at first I could see nothing. But as my eyes adjusted I saw a crippled girl lying there. She was on a pallet. Her legs were terribly twisted beneath her. Again, I felt that powerful love of Jesus coming from me toward her.

"I told her about Jesus. I told her how you had prayed for me to receive the Holy Spirit. Then I told her that I could not do a miracle, but Jesus Christ could do what is impossible for us. So then, I laid my hands on her and started to pray. As I began to pray we heard a popping and cracking sound. I did not know what it was at first, but then I saw that the girl's legs were straightening out before our eyes. That's when I realized that it was the sound of her bones popping and cracking.

"The woman who was with me screamed and ran from the hut to tell the whole village. They came running together. In the meantime, I helped the girl to her feet. She was crying. She stood for the first time in her life, and walked with me from that hut. The chief was there to see her as she came out. The whole village had assembled. Even my family had come.

"You cannot imagine the shouting, the screaming, and the dancing that started then. At last, the chief quieted them down and had me speak to the people. I told them how you had prayed for me to receive the Holy Spirit, and now I was able to see people healed in Jesus' name.

"At that moment, the chief announced that he would host a week of meetings in the village kraal. He sent runners to all the tribal villages, commanding them to come and hear the Gospel. I have been preaching and praying for the sick every day since then."

"You are the one," I said. "David, I had no idea that you were the boy they have been telling me about. Reports are running all over South Africa that God has been using a boy to bring revival among the tribes. This is glorious."

"Yes," David replied, "People are accepting Jesus everywhere I go."

"But David," I asked, "what do you preach? You told me that you only accepted Jesus as your Savior in my tent meeting that night. You have not been to Bible school. Where do you get your sermons?" I feared that he might have begun to preach a mixture of Christianity and animism. It is a common heresy in Africa.

He smiled. "I preach everything that I heard you preach."

I said, "If you preach what I preached, then thank God, you have preached the Gospel. What are you doing with the new converts?"

"Pastors are coming to baptize them after I preach. Their churches are growing fast with new people. They are happy. I want to thank you, Moruti Bonnke, for laying your hands on me, and praying for me to receive the Holy Spirit."

"You are most welcome. Praying for you in the field that night was obviously a divine appointment."

After he had gone, Anni and I reflected on his marvelous story. I felt an odd kinship with him. I was reminded that I had been just a boy in Germany when I received the baptism of the Holy Spirit in my father's Pentecostal church. In 1950, at the age of ten, I had received a call to preach in Africa. For many years, my father and mother did not take that call seriously. I was so young. But, just as David had broken with his tribal traditions in order to pray for the woman's child and see God's power, I had also come to places in my walk with God where I had been forced to step out and obey Him in spite of my family's resistance.

In one particular case, I was caught in a direct conflict between my heavenly Father and my earthly father. I remembered hearing God tell me to pray for a certain sick woman in the church where my father was ministering. I was so afraid of displeasing him. To avoid his eyes, I crawled on my hands and knees behind the pews until I reached the place where the sick woman sat. I obeyed the Lord, placing my hands on the woman and praying quietly for her. She was instantly healed and made quite a commotion in the service, telling my father what I had done. I could no longer hide. I confessed to my father, with fear and trembling. He was slow to accept the fact that God was working mightily in a mere boy.

In both cases, David's and mine, we had not acted out of rebellion. We had respected those in authority over us, but we were brought to a place where we had to respect God more. It reminds me of the time recorded in the Gospels, when Jesus' own mother and brothers came looking for Him. He ignored them, telling the crowd that anyone who did the will of His heavenly Father was His brother and sister and mother. Somehow, I believe this transition between obeying earthly authority and obeying God's authority is an essential test for those who serve Him.

In 1967, after attending Bible School in England, and pastoring in Germany, Anni and I had been assigned as missionaries to South Africa. We arrived with a passion to preach to masses of spiritually hungry Africans. But at first, we found ourselves serving white churches in a country that observed the strict separation of the races called apartheid. I was instructed not to call black believers "brother" or "sister," and I was not permitted to shake hands with them, let alone embrace them.

I was often invited to preach in white churches because they liked my ministry. This was not a common invitation for a young missionary in those days, and I must confess that I was flattered by it. At one point, I was invited to become pastor of the largest white church in all of South Africa. Such an honor! But this brought the issue of God's call on my life to a crisis point. I refused the offer saying that from the age of ten, I had not been called to preach the Gospel to whites in Africa. There had been whites enough in Germany.

Following that, I was assigned to a small mission station in the remote Kingdom of Lesotho. My family and I moved to live among black Africans. Here, I could call them "brother" and "sister," I could shake their hands and embrace them without offending the traditions of apartheid.

But at the mission station in Lesotho, I found only five people willing to listen to my sermons on a given Sunday. Obeying the Great Commission, I went beyond the walls of the church to preach to the people. I took my piano accordion to bus stops and marketplaces, and I didn't wait for Sunday to do it. I played and sang until I attracted a crowd. Then I grabbed my Bible and began to preach to the people who had come to hear the music. These years in Lesotho had further revealed that my true calling was the calling of an evangelist.

I wondered what had pushed David past the strong tribal taboos that he had respected. What had caused him to ask to pray for the woman's sick child? He had said it himself; it was an overwhelming feeling of love. This too, had been the force that had moved me past all the expectations others had placed on me. I called it compassion, the love of Christ, the call of God. It was so much more than sympathy, or empathy, or affection. It came from the indwelling person of the Holy Spirit. David's description of God's irresistible love seemed to fit my experience of this divine compassion. In these things, I identified with the tribal boy from the Transvaal.

I would like to have ended this story here. If I answered only to myself, I might have done so. But I feel the Lord urging me on. The truth about David must surely contain some lesson that is more important than a feel-good ending. I have it from several reliable witnesses that David has left his tribal homeland in the north, and has lost himself in the impenetrable slums of Soweto. He does not fellowship with the people of God anymore, and he no longer walks with the Lord.

This must serve as a warning to each of us. No matter how the power of God has been demonstrated in our lives, we can choose to walk away from fellowship with Him. Let him who thinks he stands take heed that he does not fall, the Scripture says.

It is, no doubt, a slow process. It must be like a frog in a kettle of water that is heated slowly to the boiling point. Many things can desensitize us to God's love. The cares of life can choke the Word and make it unfruitful, Jesus warned in His Parable. For someone like David, there must have been failures, disappointments, discouragements, setbacks, trials, tests, temptations – these things come to all of us. But we must choose everyday to take up our cross and follow Him, or one day any of us could find ourselves like the Prodigal. We could wake up spiritually bankrupt, living in our own pigpen, wondering how we got there.

Recently, I took a drive through Soweto. I like to travel by car and mingle with the people of a city where I am about to preach. But on this occasion, I had no preaching to do. I was just driving, looking for David. Not that I expected to find him. That would be like finding the needle in the haystack. Still I drove with an ache in my heart, and as I drove, night fell.

I thought to myself, what would I say if David suddenly appeared in the beams of my headlights? He would be forty-five years old. Would I even know him? How would I respond?

My answer was not long in coming. I would leap from the car and run to him, putting my arms around him. I would assure him that the love of God is the same today as it was on that dark night in 1977. He can begin again. And I would like to help him on that journey to restoration.

If he gave me enough time, I would encourage him with the story of Peter who returned to the Sea of Galilee to take up the vocation of fishing, after denying three times that he knew Jesus on the night of His crucifixion. Even the resurrection had not erased his shame. Jesus didn't scold him, didn't condemn him – He went and found him.

Jesus came along the shore and filled Peter's nets with fish so that he would remember the Lord's original call, "Follow Me, and I will make you fishers of men." Then He cooked him a meal on the shore and broke bread with him. As they were eating, Jesus asked him three times if he loved Him. Three questions for the man who had made three denials. Peter got the point. The breaking of Peter's heart was a good and necessary thing. Peter finally admitted the truth; his love for the Lord was not worthy to be compared to the love that Christ had shown him. That was the end and the beginning of it. That confession qualified the Big Fisherman to return to the ministry.

"Feed My sheep," Jesus said.

"Go and do likewise," I'd say to David.

❧

*The Holy Spirit does not possess us. He honors our choices.
He indwells us, and prompts us with such things as an
upwelling of divine compassion. This is what led young
David to see miraculous healings. I think we must
somehow learn to follow the prompting of compassion.
God is in it.*

CHAPTER FOUR

DIAMONDS AND DISCO DANCING

I was still a young missionary, not yet known as an evangelist, and we were just beginning to see a breakthrough in the Kingdom of Lesotho. News of our success was being talked about in the region. The year was 1973.

My phone rang. Howard Horn, someone I had known since my apprenticeship in South Africa, said, "Reinhard, come to Kimberley and preach to us.

I said, "I will come."

Kimberley was a town of about 100,000 residents, located 150 miles to the west. Like Maseru, where I lived, Kimberley was an isolated mountain community. For a century it had been famous for its diamond mines. The world's largest diamonds had come from there. The entire area was steeped in the lore of fortunes mined from the earth. Mining continued to be the backbone of the economy.

The Kimberley mines were owned and operated by the descendants of white settlers. However, the backbreaking toil in the mines was performed by black men, many of them from my own country of Lesotho. The church that I would visit in Kimberley, however, was a "whites only" congregation.

When I arrived, I remember it was a cold evening. The skies were patchy with clouds, and a chilly wind gusted from the peaks around us. Howard drove me to the church where I was to preach. We had agreed to a Friday, Saturday, and Sunday series of meetings.

That first Friday night as I sat on the platform I looked across a gathering of 200 people. Not one young person did I see in the room. Not one.

I leaned over to Howard, who was near to me, and asked, "Where are the young people?"

He nodded sadly, acknowledging that I had correctly seen the problem. Every head in the room was gray.

I preached. The service was closed, and the people filtered out to their cars to go home. When they had gone, Howard came to me.

"Reinhard, would you like to see the answer to your question? Would you like to know where all the young people in Kimberley are?"

"Yes, I would," I replied.

"I will show you. Get into my car and I will take you there."

"Where are you taking me?"

"It's a surprise," he said. He remained mysterious about it.

He drove through the streets turning this way and that until he came to a large building at the edge of a warehouse district. The building was ablaze with gaudy neon signs. One large sign blinked out the word, *disco, disco, disco.*

The parking lot was jam-packed to overflowing with vehicles. We parked on the street a block away. As he turned off the key, I could hear the boom, boom, boom, of the heavy base beat coming through the walls of that building. The so-called music seemed to shake the very ground beneath us with an ungodly spirit.

"This is a den of iniquity," I said sadly. "How awful. This is where the young people have gone?"

He nodded. "This is the latest thing, Reinhard. It is called a discotheque, a dance club. It is a craze that is sweeping the whole world right now, and young people everywhere are very attracted to it."

I felt a shiver go down my spine. How could the church compete for the attention of their youth against such temptation? The quiet little church building we had just come from, and this pulsating, giant warehouse could not seem more opposite. The disco was so large, so energetic, so loud, and so overwhelming.

Again, I could see the faces of the old people I had preached to just an hour ago. They had all come to hear Reinhard Bonnke preach to a room with no young people in it. Now they were, no doubt, sitting at home in houses with no young people in them. The young people were here, indulging in all sorts of sensual pleasures. At least they could feel confident that their parents and grandparents would not disturb them here. The older generation would not dare to enter this jarring and frightening atmosphere.

Howard got out and stood for a while leaning against the hood of his car, listening. I got out too, and stood next to him.

We could hear the music now, above the booming bass, although I couldn't really call it music. I thought of how gently I played my piano accordion, singing happy songs about Jesus to attract crowds on the streets of Lesotho. The sound of my little accordion here would have been totally drowned out. No one could have taken any notice at all. I began to feel small and insignificant.

"What do the young people see in this disco, Howard?" I asked.

He shook his head, mystified. "I don't know. I truly don't know."

After a while, he said, "Let's go inside."

"Oh, no," I said. "Let's go home. I have never gone to such a place. It would be an abomination to me. I would not know how to act. And what would people think of me as a preacher? It's unthinkable."

To this moment, I had gone along with Howard simply out of curiosity. "*Where were the young people?*" I had asked. Now I knew. It was a sad reality of modern life, but I could do nothing to fix the gulf between young and old in Kimberley, nor anywhere else in the world. Only a revival of faith in Jesus could do that.

I would go back and preach my heart out to the old people again on Saturday and Sunday. Perhaps God would move on their hearts, and they would begin to make a difference in the lives of their own young people. That seemed the best I could hope to achieve.

But as I turned to get into the car I felt bad inside. I stopped in my tracks. This is when the Holy Spirit began to speak to me. Since I had come this far, something seemed wrong if I now turned away. But I had no idea what the Spirit wanted me to do. I just couldn't leave.

"Let's take a look inside," Howard suggested.

Suddenly, this seemed exactly right. Everything in my spirit said yes. I nodded. "OK, let's just take a look at this disco."

We began to walk toward the building. What would I do? I had no idea. It was against everything in my body and my mind, but not against my spirit. I simply obeyed. We came to the door and stood there. I felt the Spirit say to me very clearly, *"Look inside. I will show you something you do not know."*

I took a deep breath, then opened the door. The blast of music must have knocked the hair back from my forehead. I have never heard such volume in my life. It was deafening. But it was in that instant that I received a spiritual vision of the reality of the disco. In the flash of the strobe lights, I did not see young people dancing with joy. I saw frozen images of boredom, fear, loneliness, and insecurity, one after the other, captured on the faces of those young people. The split-second flashes of light revealed these images, over and over and over again, like stop-action. Each of those haunted faces spoke to me of emptiness. Pure emptiness.

Now I knew what the Spirit had wanted me to know. It was not what I had expected to see. These young people were coming to the disco seeking something they did not find. No matter how they threw themselves into the beat of the music, it always came out the same – empty.

I understood in that moment that I had what they were looking for. I could show them the way to a relationship with God through Jesus Christ. I could show them the power to live a life of joy in spite of the world's many disappointments. But all of the blessings of life in Jesus would never come to them in a disco, no matter how many dance tunes they pounded out. And how would they hear the truth without a preacher? No preacher would be caught dead in this place.

Rom 10:9-10

Curiosity was gone. In its place, I felt the undeniable compassion of Jesus surging within me. I wanted to weep for the precious searching young people of Kimberley. They lived in a city that was diamond crazy. They did not know that they were the diamonds God sought. They were more precious in His sight than mountains of wealth. He cared enough to die for them.

Suddenly, I could not care less what anyone thought of me. I knew that I would preach in this disco. Nothing could deny the love of Jesus that I felt.

I shut the door and looked at Howard. I heard the Holy Spirit say in my heart, "*Find the owner of this place.*" And so, I said to Howard, "Help me to find the owner of this disco."

"What good will that do?"

"I must talk to him. Let's find him now."

"But what will you say to him?"

"I will ask him to let me preach in his disco."

Howard laughed. "You won't do that, Reinhard."

"I will. I absolutely will."

Howard followed me now. I inquired inside the disco and we were led to an office at the rear of the building. The owner was a middle-aged businessman who looked to be very much a part of the rock-and-roll culture. He had long hair, gold chains around his neck, an open collared shirt, and blue jeans.

I said to him, "Sir, I've come all the way from Germany. I am asking you for permission to allow me to address the young people in your disco for just five minutes."

He looked at me from top to toe. "You're a preacher," he said.

I was still dressed in my suit and tie. I looked like I had just come from church. I nodded.

He said, "If you want to preach you should preach in a church."

"There are no young people in the church," I said. "They don't come to the church so the preacher comes to the young people. Now give me five minutes, only five minutes, I ask of you."

"You've got to be kidding." He shook his head in disbelief, then turned around and walked away. "There is no way, man." He had no sympathy for my plea at all.

As he was walking, suddenly the Holy Spirit touched me. He said to me, *"Tell him what you saw when you looked into his dance hall."* I went after the man and took him by the arm. He turned to face me again.

"One question, sir," I said, looking deep into his eyes. "Do you think the young people find what they need for life in your disco?"

Slowly the face of that man changed. He looked down thoughtfully. When he looked up again he said, "It is very strange that you should say that. I have children of my own. I've thought many times that the disco will not give the young people what they need for life."

"I beg you, sir, give me five minutes."

He was thoughtful for a moment. "OK, but not tonight. Saturday night, tomorrow night at midnight, I will give you the microphone for five minutes."

I grabbed his hand and shook it. "It's a deal, and thank you, sir. I will be here."

I was so happy I could have kissed him. I could feel the Holy Spirit in the whole thing that was happening. It was something I would never have thought of on my own.

As Howard drove me to my room, I began to beat myself up a little bit. I had only asked for five minutes. How could I be so stupid?

I started to pray. I said, "Lord, I foolishly asked for only five minutes. Now I am stuck with five minutes because I put that number in his head. Why did I say that?" After riding some more in silence, I prayed again, a bit better this time. "Lord," I said, "nothing is too hard for You. You created the world in six days; You can save the disco in five minutes. Please do not let my foolishness be a problem. Amen." All that night I tossed and turned, and prayed. I prayed and prayed.

The next night I preached to the old people at the church. I remember nothing. I think I must have preached badly because my heart was pounding with anticipation for preaching to the lost in the disco that night. When the congregation had gone home to their houses, I asked Howard to drive me back to my room. I undressed from my suit and dressed in casual clothes. I did not want to look like a preacher just coming from church. I needed disco camouflage. Howard went home and quickly changed his clothes, too.

As we got in his car he paused to look at me. "Reinhard Bonnke, what do you think the people of the church would think if they knew where you were going tonight?"

"I think they would never come to hear me again," I said. "You won't tell them, will you?"

He smiled and shook his head. "No, of course not."

"Nor will I."

We drove to the disco, arriving at 11:30 p.m.. I had a half hour to wait. The parking lot was even more crowded on Saturday than it had been on Friday. I guess in Kimberley they had what you call "Saturday night fever." I took my Bible under my arm and my piano accordion. I don't know why I took the piano accordion, but there it was. I took it with me into that disco like a security blanket.

Inside, it was insanely crowded. Shoulder to shoulder, we had to push our way between the people to get past them to find a place to sit. Finally we came to a bar with a stool. I sat on the stool and waited for midnight.

When at last the clock struck twelve, the music stopped. I jumped up and onto the stage where the records were being spun. I took the microphone from the disk jockey and shouted, "Sit down, sit down, sit down. I've come all the way from Germany, and I've got something very important to tell you."

Suddenly, the young people began sitting down everywhere. It was then that I realized I was not in church but in a dance hall. There were no pews. Only a few bar stools at the perimeter. Most of the young people plopped right down on the dance floor. There they sat, smoking cigarettes and chewing gum, waiting for me to begin.

I started to preach one minute, two minutes, suddenly the Holy Spirit was there; I mean, the wind of God was moving in that disco. Suddenly I hear sobbing. I see young people getting out their handkerchiefs and starting to wipe their eyes, crying everywhere. And I know one thing – when people start shedding tears, it's time for the altar call. And I knew my time was flying.

I said, "How many of you want to receive Jesus Christ as your Savior? How many want to find forgiveness for your sins and enter God's plan for your life, as of tonight?"

Every hand that I could see in that place went straight up. I said, "Alright, repeat after me."

We prayed the prayer of salvation together. My five minutes were up. My work was done. I left walking on cloud number nine, rejoicing, absolutely rejoicing that I had been privileged to help these young people find what they would never find in their disco.

A year later I returned to Kimberley. Howard met me at the airport. He said, "Get in my car. I have a surprise for you."

I got in his car. He did not say anything about it; he just drove through the winding streets until he came to the warehouse district. The car stopped. I looked out of the window. I couldn't believe my eyes. I wiped them and looked again. Instead of seeing the big disco sign, there was a huge white cross on the front of that building.

"This is not the surprise," Howard said. "Come with me."

We walked up to that door where we had stood one year ago, the door that the Holy Spirit had told me to open. I remembered the pounding beat of the music that had assaulted my ears as we stood there that Saturday night. Now I heard another sound coming from inside. It was a kind of chant, growing in volume.

"Are you ready for this, Reinhard?" Howard swung the door open, and I looked into a packed house full of young people. They were chanting, "Bonnke, Bonnke, Bonnke."

I cried out with joy. They rushed to me, hugging me and shaking my hands, bringing me inside.

One young man said, "Remember me? I was the disk jockey that night that you came."

Another grabbed my hand. "I was operating the light show."

Another said, "We were dancing the night away. Now we are serving Jesus."

"After you left town, the disco went bankrupt," Howard shouted to me. "This disco is a church!" He was beaming from ear to ear.

A fine looking gentleman came up to me. "We heard about what happened to the young people here. My church has sponsored me to be a pastor to these kids."

I stood again on that disco stage looking at those faces, so different from the ones I had seen in the strobe lights a year ago. The lights were up full now. Even more, the light of the Lord's favor was shining on every face.

I pointed my finger to the heavens and shouted, "Jesus!"

"*Jesus!*" they shouted back to me as one, making the walls tremble.

"Praise Jesus!"

"*Praise Jesus!*"

"He is Lord!"

"*He is Lord!*"

"Hallelujah!"

"*Hallelujah!*"

Now that disco was rocking the right way. Kimberley's true diamonds were shining in their Father's eyes.

We must learn to hear His voice and we must learn to obey it. Not the voice of dull religion. Not the voice of our fears and prejudices. Jesus will send us to where the lost ones are, and He doesn't care if it makes us uncomfortable. It is always an adventure to follow His lead, seeking and saving the lost.

CHAPTER FIVE

PS 107

THE BONDAGE BREAKER

In 1970, I was a struggling young missionary in Lesotho, Africa. Some times only five people would show up to hear me preach. Rather than labor in an empty room, I went where the people were. In the capital city of Maseru, where I lived, I would preach four times a day in the markets, at bus stops, and in schools. This story took place during that early time of my ministry.

Dolphin Monese was a bright young student in Maseru. He had a big, happy smile and flashing brown eyes. But when he argued, his brows would knit and his jaw would clench. He looked like he took his arguments very seriously.

Dolphin studied the teachings of the Jehovah's Witnesses. He liked the way they attacked the Christian Church. The Church in the Kingdom of Lesotho had become weak and ineffective. Rather than follow a dead Christian religion, Dolphin attacked it. That was his way. In Maseru, he had become a Jehovah's Witness champion.

He walked to school each day with a group of friends. They would discuss the great issues of life, and he would impress them with his knowledge. One day, as they walked along, they saw a blind man at a bus stop playing a piano-accordion for money. Dolphin wanted to take a closer look, especially since the blind beggar was a white man. But as he came close, Dolphin could see that the man was not blind and was not a beggar. He was singing happy songs of praise to Jesus in the local Sesotho dialect. *The man is a simpleton,* he thought.

Suddenly, the man put down his piano-accordion, picked up his Bible and began to preach. One of the men in the crowd began to interpret for him. It was a trick. The man had used his music to attract people out of sympathy. *The simpleton was clever, at least,* Dolphin thought. He knew that it was not easy to gather a crowd in Maseru to hear preaching.

No problem. Dolphin had read many books about the Bible. He knew that Christians considered Jesus to be equal with God, a part of what they called the Trinity. Since he could easily defeat these silly doctrines, he would listen to the preacher's message, then argue to set him straight. It would provide amusement, and another way to impress his friends.

As you might have guessed, I was the blind beggar on the street corner that day, preaching my heart out. My work in Maseru had been fruitful only on occasion. For example, at the end of my very first sermon at a bus stop in Maseru, a tall, thoughtful young man stepped forward. I'll never forget him; his name was Michael Kolisang. He wore a colorful blanket wrapped around his shoulders. It was the popular fashion for Basuto tribesmen. He spoke to me through my interpreter. "I want this Jesus you have just preached. I want him."

What better response could I ever want to a sermon? "I want this Jesus you have just preached." I thought, maybe it will be this way everyday in Maseru! Little did I know it was beginner's luck. Pardon the expression. After that day, I preached many sermons and saw no response.

I took him into the front seat of my Volkswagen minibus. With the interpreter helping from the backseat, I led him through the salvation scriptures. Then I prayed with him to accept Jesus as his Savior. Michael Kolisang has been at my side ever since. He is today a Bishop in Lesotho, pastoring a thriving congregation.

But responses like that were few. Dolphin Monese was more typical. As soon as I finished my sermon that day, he stepped forward, not to accept Jesus, but to argue with me. Since he spoke English, he was able to argue without an interpreter.

My interpreter was happy for the break. He said that he had never worked so hard for a preacher in his life. I wore him out with four sermons per day, and he wanted a raise in pay.

Dolphin jumped into his Jehovah's Witness arguments headlong. I just smiled and listened. I knew that I could not change the young man's mind by meeting him on some battlefield of the mind. I invited him to sit down with me on the curb. He did, but he never let up.

I knew that deep inside, Dolphin was worn out by the demands of his own arguments. But I didn't know if he was tired enough to let go of them. He seemed to like arguing so much. He went on and on with his attack on Christianity until all of the crowd that had gathered that day had gone away. Even his friends had departed. It was the two of us sitting on that street curb, and only one was talking.

"May I say something?" I asked.

He was in the middle of a thought and had to finish it before he could stop himself. At last he paused. "Yes. What is it?"

"I want to say how God loves you. You and me and everyone in the world were born in sin. We were bound for eternal Hell, yet He loved us enough to…"

"There is no Hell," he interrupted. "Punishment in Hell is an idea the Popes made up. They did it to make people afraid so that they could control them. I'm not falling for any of that."

"You will have to argue with the Scripture, Dolphin. Eternal torment is clearly in the Bible. The Popes did not make it up. But that's not the Good News. The Good News is that God loved the world, even in its sin, and gave His only Son as a sacrifice for us. Salvation is a free gift, paid for by someone else. We cannot earn it by being smart, or by learning all the right things, or by doing all the right things. When we accept God's great gift, He fills us with love and peace, and we are promised eternal life with Him in Heaven. Have you accepted Jesus as your Savior?"

Dolphin went away promising he would come back to complete the correction of my bad theology. I welcomed him to return, but I must say, inwardly, I hesitated. I knew he would take advantage of my open door.

And he did. He returned every day after that. His school breaks were timed so that he could come hear me at the bus stop. Then his after-school walk brought him by my market location for another sermon. He would start more arguments. This pattern continued day after day.

In time, I found the opportunity to counter most of his arguments from Scripture. But still, this was not enough to convert him. He came again and again to argue, and perhaps for other reasons he would not admit to me. He was a tough nut to crack.

One day as I preached I sensed a powerful anointing and presence of the Holy Spirit. After my sermon that day Dolphin stepped forward.

"I am ready to accept Jesus Christ as my Savior," he said.

Amazement, almost disbelief, leapt up in my heart. This was an incredible moment. Suddenly, this young man who had come to argue had no arguments.

In that moment the Holy Spirit whispered inside of me, telling me what to do. I sensed in my inner conversation with the Lord that Dolphin must not just make a decision for Christ; he must make a clean break with the Jehovah's Witnesses at the same time. This was a source of bondage that still remained for him.

"Get in my car," I said.

He did. When we were inside I said to him, "We will drive to your house and burn all your Jehovah's Witness books. Are you ready to do that?"

Immediately, Dolphin had an inner struggle. So much of his knowledge was bound up in those books. They had given him pride and a place in the world. They had made him feel superior. I thought that if I did not place a clear choice before him, he would go into a time of struggle that would last for a long time before he would finally be free. Years of unfruitfulness could follow.

"Choose Jesus or Jehovah's Witnesses," I said. "This is the choice you make. Not two ways, just one."

At last he nodded. "Yes, you are right. Let's get the books."

This was a sign to me that the Spirit of Jesus had entered his heart. He was opening himself up to its cleansing power. By burning these books, he was burning bridges to his past – bridges that the Devil would have loved to have kept under constant traffic, back and forth, back and forth, between Jesus and Jehovah's Witnesses for unnumbered days ahead.

I drove to his house. He went inside and brought out an armful of books, depositing them in my Volkswagen minibus.

"Are these all of them?"

"I have another shelf of books at my grandma's house in the village."

"We will go there and get them. Get in, I'll drive."

"But I don't own those books. They're borrowed."

"I will pay for the books you borrowed. But we will burn them all today, borrowed or not."

Dolphin agreed. He gathered all the books from the village together and put them in the car. I purchased a gallon container of gasoline. We drove to his brother's house where he knew he could find a barrel for burning. I had him place the books inside. We doused them with the fuel.

I handed him the match. When he lit it and dropped it into the barrel an explosion of flame leapt into the air. I felt a great sense of relief. As the books burned, I could see a new Dolphin Monese emerge. The burden of carrying a heavy religious yoke was exchanged for the easy yoke and the light burden of life in Jesus Christ. Joy, peace, gentleness, meekness – all the fruit of the Spirit came pouring forth.

In the years that followed, Dolphin grew in his faith. I asked him to be my interpreter on many occasions, and he learned much about preaching and ministering through this process. He went on to Bible school. Today he is the pastor of a wonderful church in Lesotho. His intellect and personality are submitted to the will of the Lord, and his winning smile and pleasant face is a joy and comfort to many thousands.

As witnesses and evangelists, we must not be clever; we must be clear. Our message is the simple Gospel, not higher consciousness. We are not helping people to get God right, but to get right with God.
The Holy Spirit alone opens hearts and minds.

CHAPTER SIX

THE TIES THAT BIND

The footbridge had no stabilizers, no supports to keep it from swaying. It stretched dangerously above a deep, rocky chasm. The walkway had been constructed of two cables with wooden slats strung between them, nothing more. There were not even handrails. To my way of thinking, this was not a proper crossing. It was a deathtrap. I would not think of stepping onto it.

It was then that I noticed a foolish soul attempting to cross. Like a high wire amateur, the man held out his arms for balance. He crept, inch by inch, toward the other side, staring down at his trembling legs and feet. The wooden walkway tipped and swayed beneath him.

I rushed to the edge of the cliff and looked over. The bottom of the gorge could not be seen. It was covered in a morning mist. The mist moved like a river through this great gash in the earth.

I looked back at the man. He had made surprising progress, bringing himself nearly halfway to the other side. In my heart, I wished him well, but suddenly, the cloud of fog rose on a thermal updraft from the canyon. It engulfed the walkway just in front of the man. He was unaware of it. His eyes were trained on his own feet. I knew as surely as I breathed that if that man stepped into the fog he would lose his equilibrium. He would fall to his death.

I rushed to the base of the bridge to see if I could rescue him. Arriving there, I could see that if I placed one foot on that rickety walkway it would totally destroy the man's balance. I could only warn him.

"Sir, stop!" I shouted. "You must stop! The fog is in front of you."

The man turned and glanced back at me. In that moment, a shaft of pain stabbed through my soul. The man was my own brother, Jürgen. Ignoring my warning, he turned quickly, and disappeared into the fog.

"Jürgen! Jürgen!" I cried.

In a moment, I heard a scream, fading, echoing below me, as he fell.

"*Reinhaaaaard!*"

I awoke. My sheets were drenched in sweat. My heart pounded in my chest. A thousand buried feelings for my brother rose up in my heart and washed over me. I wanted to weep aloud for Jürgen. I knew that he had wandered far from Jesus.

"Lord, what is this I have seen?"

The answer was clear and specific: *"Jürgen is on the bridge to eternity. If you don't warn the godless, I will require his blood at your hand."*

I objected. "Lord, this makes no sense. I know Jürgen is far from You, but how should I warn him when he knows the way of salvation as well as I do?" *"If you don't warn the godless, I will require his blood at your hand."*

Why did I question God? I don't know. Perhaps I reacted like the Virgin Mary when the angel Gabriel announced that she would have a baby. It made no sense to her natural mind. She said, "Lord, how will this happen since I have never known a man?" This is not a question of unbelief, but a question of how best to obey Him.

Likewise, the Lord's instructions to me made no sense. But how well I knew that everything good in my life, every ounce of fruitfulness, had come from simple obedience to His voice, not from argument. I began to obey Him as a ten-year-old child, and I've never improved on that kind of obedience. But as an adult, I sometimes ask questions, and I share that with you here because, chances are, you do too. God speaks, and your natural mind balks at His words in your heart. It is okay to ask Him about it.

I suppose that I tell about my questioning the Lord for three good reasons. First, because you need to know that we are all alike – what is possible for me is possible for you, both for the good and for the bad. Also, because I have found that this is a lesson that is not learned just once. We are human. We slip back into our natural way of thinking every day. Finally, because even though I argued, I eventually did obey the voice of the Spirit. In the parable of the two sons In Matthew 21, Jesus praised the son who said "no" to his father, but later reconsidered and obeyed. He condemned the one who agreed quickly, but never did obey his father's voice.

This story reveals an important lesson. If you have not obeyed the still, small voice of the Holy Spirit speaking in your heart, it is not too late. You can begin today, and again tomorrow, and again the day after that. His mercies are new every morning.

My memories of Jürgen immediately took me back to our childhood. We were two of six children, born to Hermann and Meta Bonnke. Before coming to know the Lord, our father had become a career soldier in the German Army. He served as a supply officer in Hitler's fortress city of Königsberg, in East Prussia. During that time, he had become deathly ill with tuberculosis. In desperation, he sought the Lord and was born again and healed of the disease at the same time.

Nothing was the same for him again. He never missed an opportunity to tell people that God had saved and healed him. Everything else that had once seemed important became worthless next to the knowledge of God. He wanted to leave the military and become a full-time minister, but he was required to finish his career in the German Army. In the meantime, he found ways to serve the Lord as a lay minister. At this time, he met and married Meta Sheffling, a church organist from Danzig, a city known today as Gdansk. That was 1933.

All six of us Bonnke children were born to Hermann and Meta between 1934 and 1942. It was a prolific span of just eight years in their marriage. During this time our family lived comfortably in the small town of Stablack.

The first five Bonnke children to be born were boys. The oldest was Martin, and then Gerhard, after that, a set of twins, Peter and Jürgen. By now, Mother felt she was finished with bearing sons. She wanted a daughter. Thirteen months later, I was born, and my mother cried. *"Please God, why not a girl?"* After me, God was merciful, and Felicitas was born in 1942, the only Bonnke daughter.

As we grew from childhood to adulthood, Felicitas and I served the Lord. The others rejected the faith of their parents.

Jürgen, Peter, and I were close in years and experience. We remember many things alike. He was nearly six, and I was five when we were forced to flee for our lives from East Prussia. Felicitas was just an infant. Mother packed us up and led the way. Our father had to stay, and do what he could to delay the Russian Army, which was beginning to overrun the region, eager to take vengeance on all German people.

Mother prayed with us that God would give us safe passage out of the war zone. After prayer, she secured a ride on a fleeing military truck that took us across the frozen sea to Gdansk. We were being bombed and strafed by the Russian Air Force along the way. The day after we made the crossing, thousands of others were plunged to an icy grave behind us, as the ice highway gave way to the force of the spring thaw, helped along by the constant pounding of the Russian military.

We had miraculously crossed through a narrow window of safety. We were horrified at what had happened to the unfortunate ones behind us. Had they prayed, too? Were their prayers not answered?

Mother prayed and read her Bible every day for guidance and protection for us. From the Scripture, she received assurance that God would preserve us on our escape route across the sea. We arranged passage to Denmark on a refugee ship, but were denied entrance at the last minute. That ship was torpedoed by a Russian submarine. It sank, killing three times more passengers than died on the Titanic. Once more, we had been spared, but what of the dead? Why not us?

The ship that we eventually took was also bombed and strafed along the way. I remember climbing to the deck and seeing a flaming Russian airplane falling from the sky above us. At one point, we were rocked by a huge explosion as we struck a mine. The ship began listing badly to one side, then, inexplicably, righted itself. We continued on until we reached safe harbor in Denmark.

News of Nazi atrocities began to come out of Germany. Hatred toward all Germans began to grow. In Denmark, we were unwelcome. For safe keeping, we were placed in an internment camp until our fate could be decided. This action spared us from death at the hands of mobs seeking to kill us in the bitter aftermath of the war.

Four years later we were repatriated to Germany and were finally reunited with Father. I was nine years old and Jürgen ten. As we entered the period of rebuilding Germany, the Bonnke clan began life as a family once more. All eight of us shared a single room in the town of Glückstadt, near Hamburg. Our household may have been poor in material goods, but we were rich in faith.

Our father, released from military duty, soon became a full-time pastor. His passion to preach the Gospel did not end at the church door. His six children heard all of his sermons preached in the course of everyday living. God was serious stuff in our house. Our family had been spared as we had fled for our lives after the war. Those stories of deliverance were often recited to instill in us the knowledge of God's power and care.

At first, all of the Bonnke children accepted our heritage in the Lord without question. We gave ourselves completely to the faith of our parents. However, as the years moved on, Martin, Gerhard, Peter, and Jürgen began to question the family faith. Even the stories of deliverance came into question. They found other natural ways to explain our escape at war's end. It was not the hand of God, they said, it was chance, luck, coincidence, fate, anything but God. Even our father's healing from tuberculosis could be explained in terms of psychology and psychosomatic symptoms, they decided.

I know that this is a familiar story. It happens in many families of faith. The Book of Judges 2:12 brings us a sad phrase from the history of God's people, repeated again and again in the Old Testament: "and they forsook the Lord, the God of their fathers, who had brought them out of the land of Egypt." This Scripture came true before my eyes as Jürgen and I grew up. My older brothers forsook the Lord. It was hurtful for me. But for my parents, I can now see that it was many times more painful.

My younger sister Felicitas and I were part of that same family, and we held to the faith of our parents until it became completely real to us. What made the difference? I don't know. But there are as many explanations as there are families.

I know that in Germany after the war there was much blaming. Everything from the older generation came under criticism. Our father's claims to God's miraculous favor were placed in the same basket with death camp discoveries and other wartime horrors. "Where was God?" the young people asked. "Did we think the Bonnkes were His favorites or something?" "What good had faith done for all the unlucky ones who had not escaped the war with their lives?"

With questions like these, my brothers rejected faith and began to worship intellect and science. They were determined never to make the same mistakes as the older generation. They saw our belief in the Lord as something easily manipulated, and they wrongly thought that by using their minds, they would live superior lives. They invested themselves in schooling as I began to invest myself in our father's church activities. Our paths went east and west.

I was now ten years old. It was at this time that I received my call to be a missionary to Africa. As I entered my teen years, I took this calling with all seriousness. My brothers, Jürgen included, really turned on me. They began to openly despise my relationship with the Lord. It was childish, they said. They ridiculed it as something for simpletons. They persecuted me as an inferior species of human being. This attitude continued right on into adulthood.

My brothers went to fine universities. They applied themselves diligently to master their chosen disciplines in the academic world. Jürgen became a highly esteemed chemical engineer. The brothers Bonnke laughed at my choice of attending a lowly Bible school. Each of them, and even Felicitas, who remained faithful, earned doctorate degrees in medicine and other sciences as I began my first humble missionary efforts with Anni in Lesotho, Africa.

During those years of building the ministry, I would sometimes travel home to Germany for a visit. Mother and Father, of course, were most proud of me. They watched from afar the beginnings of Christ for all Nations, and had even visited our African crusades, overwhelmed to see the responses. But for many years, my brothers continued to ridicule the work.

My heart would hurt as I saw millions of decisions for Christ around the world, and would come home to find that my own brothers were still completely hardened to the Gospel of Jesus.

Jürgen's house had become the place I least enjoyed to visit. He had married a woman who was a secretary. She thought of herself as highly intelligent. Christian faith was something to be ridiculed and attacked. She remained completely hostile to the Gospel. When I visited, she would become aggressive, constantly challenging me to answer questions about the failure of the Christian faith. She attacked me with so much vigor that Jürgen was put to shame. I could tell that he loved me as a brother, even if he looked down on my life of ministry. He could gently oppose me, but did not want the conflict to become so mean.

When visiting Jürgen's house, and all of my brothers' houses, I took the "soft answer turns away wrath" approach. I stopped talking of things that I knew would rile their emotions. Instead, I spoke in more general terms, and I spent more time and effort listening. Since we all shared the same Gospel-filled childhood, I believed that I should win them with sugar, not with confrontation. This approach had borne some fruit.

My brothers and I, including Jürgen and his wife, were together in the mid-1980s for a family reunion. We would sit each day at mealtime around a long table and share conversation.

I believe it was my brother, Martin, who started this particular conversation. He is my oldest brother, and is a doctor of chemistry. He said that the name Bonnke was all over the newspapers in Germany thanks to me. Reporters, he said, flew to my crusades around the world to report back in Germany on what was happening. Their reports included some fantastic accounts of miraculous healings. This, he said, had created a problem for him. The name Bonnke was rare in Germany, and people were now calling him thinking that he was me.

"As you know," he said, "my name is in the phone book in the Frankfurt area. Recently my phone rang."

"Dr. Bonnke?" It was a woman's voice.

I said, "Yes, I am Dr. Bonnke."

She said, "Dr. Bonnke, I am sick with cancer. Heal me! Would you please heal me?"

I said, "Lady, I can't heal anyone, I'm not a medical doctor. I'm a chemist. I can make medicine, but I can't heal anyone."

She said, "Your name is Bonnke? B-o-n-n-k-e?"

I said, "Yes, Bonnke."

She said, "You are Bonnke, heal me! Please!"

I said, "Lady, you want my brother Reinhard. But let me tell you something; he doesn't heal anybody either. Jesus does."

I could not contain my laughter. "Oh, Martin," I replied, "are you now preaching the Gospel?"

It was a fine moment. My brother's story had broken through a lot of the old tension. It was good to know that he was finding a way to acknowledge me in front of the others.

But Martin was not finished. He then said that he had an announcement to make. He said that he and the brothers had evaluated the lives of all the Bonnke children, and between them had voted me "best horse in the stable." He quickly added that this honor was strictly about my impact in the world, not about whether it had been for good or ill.

Still, this was a big step. They had for many years ridiculed all of the things that now made me, in their own words, "best horse in the stable."

It gave me hope that one day they might take the next step and acknowledge that my life had impact because of Jesus Christ, and for no other reason, and that they once again accepted his Lordship in their lives. By this gesture, I could see that the animosity between us had been replaced by real affection, even though we did not share the same living faith.

So, after waking up from my dream about Jürgen, I presented this case to the Lord: "Lord, see the progress we have made with sugar, not with sermons? Why do You now tell me, 'If you don't warn the godless, I will require his blood at your hand?' What do You mean? Am I to preach him the sermon that he has heard a thousand times? Will he learn anything new if I now tell him he is a sinner and bound for Hell? I don't understand."

The Lord replied to me, *"Write him a letter and tell him what you saw in the dream."*

This sounded like God speaking. "I will do it, Lord," I said. And I turned over, and went back to sleep.

The year was 1985. At this time in my ministry, I had begun planning to move Christ for all Nations from Johannesburg to Frankfurt. It was a huge move. We would lose most of the prayer partners and supporters we had won in South Africa over a full decade of ministry there. God had widened the Christ for all Nations river through these people so that we could have maneuverability. But this maneuver seemed like it would narrow our channel again, just when we needed to step out and do greater things for God. I was trusting that I had heard Him correctly. Many confirmations had already come.

For one thing, the Apartheid policy of South Africa had become a liability to our work. Some countries were working against us because of it. We were being painted with the racist brush simply because of our address. The Lord showed me that a German passport would allow my team to move freely in countries that were diplomatically opposed to us at the time. The Lord's leading, as always, is more than strategic. I am amazed looking back on this.

So, as I got up from bed to start my day, I continued the intense planning for this major move to Germany. In the middle of my work, I heard the voice of the Spirit, clearly in my heart. *"You didn't write the letter. I will require his blood at your hands."*

I stopped everything. I wrote that letter, telling Jürgen what I had seen in the dream. I sent it. I did not hear a reply. I went on with life and forgot about it.

We moved to Germany. Anni and I made ready our new residence to receive our children home on visit from the university. They arrived, and we had prepared dinner. Just as we were sitting down to eat, I was handed a letter addressed to me from Jürgen. I opened it and read:

Dear Reinhard,
    My wife left me. My best friend died of cancer. I was so frustrated I thought life was not worth living. I wanted to kill myself. But in the night I had a dream. I was walking on a bridge. It had no handrails and I fell down and screamed as I fell. I woke up, sweating with fear. I jumped out of bed

and said, "Almighty God, You know that I don't even believe in You, but I have a brother who serves You. If You have spoken to me through this dream, speak to me through Reinhard." Sometime later, your letter came. Your dream was my dream. I have given my life to Jesus. He has forgiven me of my sins.

Even in front of my children, I broke down and cried like a baby. I could not help myself, and no one could eat for some time after that. This kind of thing prostrates my soul, and leaves me speechless before the King of kings and Lord of lords.

The ties that bind a family together must surely mean more in the Spirit than we can know in the flesh. God can link us together, though we are 5,000 miles apart, causing us to dream the same dream. This is so much more than coincidence. God spoke in the still, small voice to me. What if I had neglected His instructions to write the dream to my brother? This story is another illustration of His infinite ways to seek and to save the lost. Oh, how He loves you and me.

Today, my brother Jürgen is saved, yet he is also a broken man. His health is gone, his mental abilities nearly wiped out. He lies in a nursing home being cared for day and night. But soon, perhaps by the time you read this story, he will be face to face with the Lord we both long to see.

I am so happy.

❧

This story reveals an important lesson. If you have not obeyed the still, small voice of the Holy Spirit speaking in your heart, it is not too late. You can begin today, and again tomorrow, and again the day after that.
His mercies are new every morning.

CHAPTER
SEVEN

THE LIONS' DEN

I flew to Kano, Nigeria in 1991. The evangelistic meetings would begin in two days. Peter van den Berg, my ministry director, and evangelist Brent Urbanowicz, one of my future sons-in-law, flew with me. At the airport, we came down the stairway and were met by the local sponsoring board of pastors.

John Darku, the crusade director, looked worried. He took me to one side. "Reinhard," he said, "you cannot go into the terminal. There are snipers who have sworn to kill you."

I looked at the terminal and could see armed soldiers standing by the windows.

"You are sure of this?"

"We are sure."

I thought John might have been overreacting. Perhaps there had been death threats and he was going the extra mile. Still, I appreciated his caution. My main concern, in this case, was not for me. I had preached under death threats before. Rather, I felt terribly responsible for the partners who would be arriving in a matter of hours from the United States and Europe. They were coming to witness the largest crowds in the history of Christ for all Nations Crusades. What had I brought them into?

"The snipers will have to get past the soldiers," I suggested.

"It can be done," John replied. "Some of the soldiers are Muslim. They might have radical sympathies."

"Okay, John. What are we to do?"

A line of cars and drivers pulled up next to us. Obviously, a plan was underway.

"The government has arranged to process your passport through back channels," he explained. "Airport authorities want you to leave through a secret entrance."

I nodded.

The three of us were put quickly into separate vehicles. I was placed in the lead car, and my driver quickly sped across the tarmac. The others followed close behind. The cars went behind a hangar, and suddenly they stopped. The drivers leaped out. They took me from my seat and exchanged me quickly with Brent, who had been in a trailing car. Then we were off again.

"Why have you done this?" I asked.

"The snipers may not know what you look like. We thought we would at least confuse them."

As we sped on, I wondered if Brent understood that he had just been made a decoy for snipers who were looking for me. I'm sure he hadn't signed up for that duty when he had proposed to my daughter.

We left the airport property and began driving an erratic route through the back streets. It was nearly dark when we arrived at our rented house. We unpacked and settled in. By telephone and two-way radio, my team monitored the arrivals of all our American and European guests. Group by group, they found their way to their accommodations in Kano without incident.

I listened to local radio news of Muslim unrest concerning our visit. I thought that underneath all the arguments, they were really upset that many Muslims would turn to Christ in our meetings, as they had done a year earlier in Kaduna. We prayed about it, committing ourselves and everyone associated with the crusade into the hands of God.

As we prepared for bed, I said to Brent, "You passed the test."

"What test?" he asked.

"You can marry my daughter."

He stopped for a moment, then laughed. "Are there going to be more tests like this one?"

"I pray not," I replied.

I laid down in the darkness, but sleep would not come. From the distance, I heard the haunting wail of a muezzin calling the Muslim faithful to prayer. Had I really heard it? Or was my imagination now running wild? I silently prayed, Lord, has my zeal for reaching Nigeria blinded me? Have I been unwise? I've brought these innocent people into danger. Protect them, Lord.

I had been zealous for Nigeria. It was home to more people than any other African nation. With a population of 140,000,000, it ranks as one of the ten most populated countries on the planet. You cannot imagine the cities that teem with people in the ten geographical regions of this landmass, stretching from the Gulf of Guinea, north, and eastward to Lake Chad. It is the very stuff of this evangelist's dreams.

However, about half of the people in Nigeria are Muslims. Most of these are concentrated in the north. Christian evangelism among Muslims is forbidden. On the other hand, Muslims seek to convert "infidels," including Christian believers. Between Christian and Muslim beliefs, the fabled immovable object meets the unstoppable force. Something must give. I tell my Muslim friends that Jesus died for Muslims, pagans, and Christians. I declare the Gospel and leave the rest up to the Holy Spirit. Nevertheless, the Muslim world presents a hostile challenge for all of us in the Body of Christ today.

In order to follow God's vision of a blood-washed Africa, I knew that sooner or later Christ for all Nations would have to penetrate Muslim strongholds in the northern part of the African continent, including Sudan, Libya, Morocco, Algeria, Chad, and Egypt. For that reason, the northern part of Nigeria represented a test case for us. It was home to the kind of fanatical Muslim resistance we would eventually meet as we pushed further north.

Rather than jump into the deep end of the pool, we started in the shallows, so to speak. It is my belief that God arranged for the boy David to face a lion and a bear before he took on Goliath of Gath. In that spirit, we held our first Nigerian crusade in 1985 in the southern city of Ibadan. It was a wonderful crusade, and we were greatly encouraged. We followed in the next four years with a series of meetings in the cities of Lagos, Onitsha, Aba, Port Harcourt, Enugu, and Warri - all located in the coastal strip along the Gulf of Guinea. Near the end of 1989, we ventured onto the country's great central plateau to the Muslim city of Jos.

The meeting went well. But we could feel the religious tension rising as our team stood poised, looking northward toward the city of Kano. It was a Muslim holy city, a walled fortress in ancient times, built by slavers.

I stopped here and took a deep breath. We would go forward with caution. My team members were in agreement that we should test the waters once more. We would first try a crusade in a lesser Muslim stronghold before entering Kano. Therefore, in 1990, we scheduled a crusade in the city of Kaduna. The population of Kaduna was nearly 70 percent Muslim. This was a huge step of faith that resulted in the greatest breakthrough we had ever seen.

The size of the crowd that greeted us in Kaduna took our breath away. For the first time in my life I looked upon a crowd of a half-million souls. All of my earlier thinking about using the world's largest tent, seating 34,000, was made completely useless by this mass of humanity. And it seemed significant to me that we first saw this happen on disputed Muslim ground.

Our team felt a huge responsibility to deliver a clear message to every lost soul in attendance. Our technicians had already put strategies in place to bring my voice effectively to such a crowd. From experience we knew that we could not allow such an important event to be at the mercy of the local power grid. We brought generators for lights, sound, computers, and other essential equipment. Nor did we trust the local weatherman. A small weather station was set up to monitor humidity, wind, pollen, ozone, and any atmospheric conditions that might affect the hearing of the Word. This information was constantly updated into a computer that would adjust the speaker relay system across the twenty-five acre crusade field.

Everything worked fantastically. God broke through. We saw miracles of healing to verify the preaching. Hundreds of thousands of Muslims came to the Lord. On the platform behind me, the sponsoring Christian pastors in that city were weeping with joy. The success of the meeting seemed pivotal. It now seemed to me that a dominant Muslim culture would not be an impossible barrier to God's promise that Africa shall be saved. I told my staff to schedule a meeting for the coming year in Kano.

As planning went forward, I enthusiastically invited partners and friends from Europe and the United States to join us. I expected the crowds in Kano to be even greater than we had seen in Kaduna. Someone had promised me in the 1980s, when we were seeing crowds of 200,000, that one day we would see 1,000,000 souls in a single crowd. It seemed unthinkable at that time. After Kaduna, I knew that this had been a true prophecy, and by God's grace we would soon see it come to pass. I thought perhaps that it would happen now, in Kano. I wanted to share this fantastic experience with those who had supported us so long and so well.

We had our first taste of difficulty, however, when we chose a public outdoor area for the meetings. At the last minute, a local mullah, a Muslim religious teacher, claimed it to be a holy site. We did not understand the connection, but in order not to offend, we agreed to seek another location.

Realizing that we might face more trouble, we took precautions. Instead of booking hotel rooms for myself and other high-profile members of the team, we secretly rented guesthouses in the outlying areas of the city. We did this for the partners we had invited from Europe and America as well, a move that was beginning to appear divinely inspired.

In time, our Kano Crusade Committee had found a Catholic compound willing to host our meetings. They gave permission to set up our platform, generators, lights, and sound equipment in a large open area within their fenced property. No Muslim claim could be made against this ground since it had clearly been a Christian enclave for decades. We had the problem of all the crusade publicity we had posted in the city. It directed traffic to the wrong area. But we would solve that problem by posting local ushers to redirect the crowds to the new location. If publicity geared up in the usual pattern for us, God would perform miracle healings, and these would make local headlines, and the spiritually hungry people of Kano would find us in record numbers.

Now I lay awake wondering if all of this thinking and planning had somehow missed the mark. And yet, I knew that God had a bigger view of our present troubles than any of us could possibly know. I went to sleep in that confidence, leaving our situation in His omnipotent hands.

The next morning after devotions, I told the men that I would like to drive through the city, as I normally do. I wanted to see the people of Kano for myself. When I preach in a new place I need to smell the air. I need to see the local activities. It helps me to get a feel for the city.

We got a car. Peter and Brent went with me. As we drove, I noticed many more mosques than churches in Kano. During our tour we drove past the local Emir's palace. The Emir is not a religious leader. He is the Muslim political leader for a region. Outside of his palace we saw a crowd of thousands of young men dressed in white robes. They had blocked the road. We drove slowly up to them, and they parted like the Red Sea to let us pass through. Many of them bent down and looked intently into the car as we moved through the crowd. I noticed that all of the young men seemed to be very angry, but we passed through without incident.

At noon we arrived back at our house. Our host met us, wringing his hands. "Kano is burning," he said. "A Muslim mob has gone on a rampage."

We looked back toward the city and could see columns of smoke rising. Reports came to us that the young men we had seen at the Emir's palace had just come from a mosque where a mullah had told them, "Bonnke must not be allowed to preach in the holy city of Kano."

How had they missed us? We had driven straight through their midst. Had the Holy Spirit simply blinded their eyes? If one of those young men had recognized my face, we would have been dragged from the car and killed on the spot. The city was covered with our crusade posters. My picture was prominently displayed everywhere. How had we escaped? Unable to find me, the mob had begun targeting Christian churches, homes, businesses, and pedestrians.

The next morning, John Darku arrived at our house with a senior Air Force officer. The officer said, "The Governor has declared a state of emergency. You must pack your things and leave now."

"Where will we go?"

"I have arranged to take you to another place," John said. "The airport is teeming with rioters. They are trying to cut off your escape route. We can't go back there. They are getting too close to this house, and you have been seen in this neighborhood. It won't be safe to stay."

"How much time do we have?" I asked.

"Five minutes," the Air Force officer said. He looked genuinely scared. "Get your things. We must go, now!"

John drove us to another house. It belonged to a precious Christian woman. When we arrived there, her children were keeping watch. They came and told us that they had seen Muslim rioters only a few blocks away.

"John," I said, "we cannot stay here. They are going to search house to house for me. I cannot bear to bring this woman and her children into such danger."

John nodded. He took us on another high-speed trip through the back streets. We arrived at the home of a local businessman. He must have been a very brave fellow to allow us to stay in his home that night.

From the roof of the house, we could see the reflection of fires flickering across the night sky. Explosions could be heard as petrol stations were set on fire, billowing huge clouds of black smoke into the air. Occasional gunfire rattled through the darkness. We were out of sight, but hardly removed from the danger zone. The entire city was being ransacked in a mad search for me. That night on the news we heard that the government had closed the airspace over Kano. This puzzled me. What did they know? Were the Muslim fanatics planning to use civilian airplanes against us? Or had some of the Air Force pilots themselves been involved in a plot? I ordered that the crusade planned for the next day would not go on.

The next morning I sent word to my team to gather at my location for prayer. We would decide what to do next. Our people came, but they told of seeing dead bodies and burned-out wreckage strewn through the streets as they drove to the meeting. Hundreds were dying. The mob was totally out of control. The local police were not able to contain them. As Christians were encountered, they were being killed.

The officer from the Air Force base came to the compound. He told us that the Army was clearing the airport, trying to secure it so that we could leave. They would provide for an emergency air evacuation. He urged us to get out as fast as we could. "They are like ants," he said. "They are swarming wherever they go. If they find this location they will soon come pouring over the property."

I asked that all of our guests from America and Europe be allowed to leave first. The military officer disagreed. He persuaded me that since I was the target of this violence, I should leave first. If it became known that I had gone, the mob might calm down and disperse. Others would be in less danger as they were being airlifted out.

"The longer you stay, the longer this violence will go on," he said.

I agreed to cooperate. Once the airport was secure, they would escort me to an airplane and announce in the news media that I had gone. I asked all of my team members to stay in the compound and join me in this evacuation. It seemed the only thing to do.

As we waited for word from the airport, I took a walk around the grounds. A feeling of grief came over me. All of the events in Kano became glaringly real. Christians were dying because I had come to town. Yet, no – it was much more than that.

Kano was burning because of the Gospel of Jesus Christ. "If the world hates you," Jesus said in John 15:18, "you know that it has hated Me before it hated you."

I looked at the street, imagining the mob swarming in our direction. *"What will I do, Lord, if suddenly they appear, demanding Reinhard Bonnke?"*

In only a moment, I knew the answer, and I felt His peace settle over me.

Peter van den Berg walked up to join me.

"Peter," I said, "if that mob shows up before they get the airport secure, I will give myself up to them. I want you to know that."

"I won't let you give yourself up."

"You must. I will identify myself, Reinhard Bonnke, an evangelist for the Lord Jesus Christ, and go out to them. That might save the others. My life is His."

"If they show up," Peter said, "I'll grab you and drag you up to the roof there. We'll both take up roof tiles and battle them to the last man, that's what we'll do!"

I grinned at him. Peter was a fighter. We had been through many adventures together on the road to a blood-washed Africa. I knew him well enough to know that he meant what he said. And he knew me well enough to know that I too meant what I said – immovable force and unstoppable object. We said no more but went back inside.

At this time, Winfried Wentland, the foreman of my crusade facilities crew, approached me. His wife, Gabrielle stood beside him. Winfried is a focused and intense man, a former German soldier of wiry build. Gabrielle, called "Gaby," is his match. If ever two people could see through the smoke of Kano to the real fire – the mission of saving souls – it was this pair. They had been with me for twelve years in Africa.

"Gaby and I believe we are supposed to stay here and bring the equipment home," Winfried said.

His words hit me like bullets. Given the way events had spiraled out of control, it was out of the question. I looked at Gaby, in her ninth month of pregnancy. I simply could not believe my ears.

"Equipment can be replaced, Winfried," I said. "You and your family cannot be replaced. I won't think of it."

"Reinhard, I have fifty men at the compound. It is my officer's training to leave no one behind. Besides, they have already risked their lives. I need to finish what we started together."

I appreciated his argument, but it didn't convince me. The fifty men were local volunteers he had recruited, and now supervised, in the setting up of the crusade grounds. I shook my head. "You can send word to the men that you will return when hostilities have ended. This only makes sense. They will surely understand. I want you and Gaby to stay with us and evacuate."

"Reinhard," he continued, "Gaby and I and the children have prayed together about this. We have heard from God and He has given us perfect peace. Look at us; we are in peace. Whether we live or die, God is going to see us through. Please do not order us to disobey the Lord."

For this, I had no argument. "I will have to think about it," I said, and walked away, too disturbed to continue. Winfried and I both knew what my answer would be. I did not want to contemplate it.

But I am human. I had questions. If God had spoken to the Wentlands, what did He have in mind? I didn't want to believe that God would do any less than He had done for us as we had driven through the mob at the Emir's palace. But I couldn't be sure of that.

In serving our crusade team, Winfried and Gaby had lived a life of adventure and risk every day. Yet they were a family, and they insisted on doing everything together – kids included. Having them on my team made me feel blessed of the Lord. But I would never have asked them to drive our equipment out of Kano under these circumstances.

I began to pray. Lord, they say that the blood of the martyrs is the seed of the church. Right now, I don't want to believe that. In Scripture I read that your Word is the seed. Jesus was the Word made flesh. He was the seed who fell into the ground and died, and you raised Him up again, victorious over death. Let us bring forth the fruit of His resurrection in Kano, Lord. Let Your Gospel prevail, and protect Winfried and Gaby, and everyone who has come to serve You in this crusade.

I knew that a week ago, Winfried had driven our crusade eighteen-wheeler from his home in Lagos, Nigeria to Kano. That is like driving seven hundred miles from Denver to Dallas on an unpaved alleyway. African roads are not for the faint of heart. The truck is equipped with six-wheel-drive for good reason. Gaby had accompanied him, as she usually did, driving their

Land Rover in convoy. Their two children, Simon and Angelina, ages nine and five, had come along.

Suddenly, I could picture them on the road. The trailer he pulled was a rolling advertisement for a blood-washed Africa. It was blood red, with massive white lettering on the side, spelling out, J-E-S-U-S. Surely it had created a stir in Muslim neighborhoods as it had been en route. I began to wish that I had painted it solid white, with no emblem on it whatsoever.

Looking at these events from the outside, Winfried and Gaby seemed unduly adventuresome. To some, they would, no doubt, appear irresponsible. But this is not so. They are ordinary believers who are responding to the challenge of following Jesus. Who knows what any of us would be empowered to do by simply hearing and obeying the Lord and subduing our fears.

As Winfried explains it, they considered the Kano assignment routine. The family had shared equally in his calling from the very start. By the time of this story, they knew Africa and its hazards well. They had seen violent clashes in other cities where they had served. Some crusades had been held in active war zones. They knew how to take precautions, but they also had few illusions, knowing that many safety factors remained beyond control. Those had to be left in God's hands.

On the first day of the rioting, Winfried had seen the smoke from his hotel room. He had taken a motorbike and hurried to the Catholic compound where the crusade platform had been set up. Inside, he found the crew of fifty Christian men he had recruited from local churches. They were worried but were taking action to protect the crusade equipment. They had closed and locked the perimeter gates and had posted men on lookout all around to warn them should the mob approach.

Indeed, soon the mob appeared. Within sight of the crusade platform stood a large petrol station with ten pumps. The mob attacked it. A huge fireball had shot into the sky. The entire station began exploding and burning. Black smoke engulfed the area.

The Christian volunteers persuaded Winfried to spend the night back at his hotel. Since the mob was seeking Bonnke, any white man seen at the compound might draw the mob inside. They assured him that they would stand guard all night. This had been Winfried's experience of the Kano situation so far.

At this time, at the home where my team waited, the Air Force officer arrived to tell us that buses were approaching to take us to the airport. I had known from the start that I would not ask Winfried to disobey anything he had heard from God. I called the two of them to join me for a time of prayer. I laid my hands on them and prayed for God's protection to surround them. I especially prayed for Gaby and the child in her womb. I asked God to assign His angels to guide and protect them until they arrived again at their home in Lagos.

As I finished the prayer, I felt saddened again. I truly feared that I had seen them for the last time. Christians were being hunted down and killed in the streets of Kano. Winfried would now travel those streets pulling a large blood-red trailer with J-E-S-U-S spelled out in block letters on the side. It would be like walking through a war zone wrapped in the enemy's flag. To me, it seemed to be a call to martyrdom.

That day, in order to begin to control the city again, the local police and military announced a "shoot on site" curfew from 6 p.m. until 6 a.m. When the curfew was in place that evening, our evacuation began. We entered a convoy of military buses with soldiers stationed at every window. The muzzles of machine guns bristled in all directions. As we entered the vehicles, we were relieved to see that all of our American and European guests were also on board. Our scattered crusade team had been collected, with the exception of Winfried and Gaby. We sped to the airport. Soon we were flying away, breathing easier aboard those rescue jets.

I thought of Winfried and his family left behind. How would they face the outcome of their decision to obey the Lord? I knew them well enough to know the answer to that question. The answer was simple. Although they were on the ministry payroll, they had never been working strictly for me. No one but God could have directed them to take this action. They were obeying. People in obedience to the Lord do not worry, do not fret, do not need to know all of the outcomes before they are willing to commit themselves. They would face Kano the way any of us would have done it – one moment at a time. Borrowing no anxiety from the future, they would simply put one foot in front of the other until they arrived – either at their earthly or their heavenly home.

Before we left, plans had been made for a contingent of soldiers to guard the Catholic compound while Winfried directed his men in the dismantling and packing of our crusade equipment. He returned with his family to the hotel that night.

At six o'clock the next morning, the curfew was lifted, and the worst violence of all erupted. Apparently my leaving the city had not appeased anyone. It only threw more fuel on the fire of a raging mob. They had been looking for an opportunity to attack infidels anyway. Their blood lust was not yet satisfied.

From the hotel balcony, Winfried and Gaby watched as more fires sprang up. They listened to even more explosions and gunfire around the city. Later in the morning, Winfried took a car and drove to the compound. His men had been able to keep the equipment secure.

During the night, however, our equipment had been discovered by a number of suspicious individuals. The men guarding the truck had taken these people into custody. They held them under lock and key in an inner building within the compound. This had been done to keep them from informing the mob of where to find Bonnke's equipment and crew.

Winfried thanked his men for their faithfulness and bravery. He said he would return the next morning with some soldiers to guard them while the equipment was being taken down and packed for the return trip. His crew pledged another fifty Christian men, one hundred in all, in order to speed the effort. Winfried had never felt more proud of a group of men in his life.

On Friday morning, five soldiers came to the hotel to escort Winfried through the streets. At the compound, they found one hundred local Christian men assembled, as promised. They were waiting for Winfried's orders. As Winfried gave them their assignments, they began the process of dismantling the platform and sound stations and packing them into the trailer.

Suddenly, a huge explosion rocked the area. The soldiers were watching the skies. Nothing appeared. Still, they had become frightened. They forced Winfried into his car and ordered him to take them to their barracks to get more soldiers.

At the barracks it soon became apparent that the men had no intentions of getting reinforcements. They went to their superior officer and insisted that the compound was about to be overrun. The mob would have its way, they said. They convinced the officer not to send them back.

Winfried thought that perhaps it was just as well that these men did not return with him. These soldiers might have been Muslims who did not wish to risk their lives under the circumstances.

At the barracks, he was approached by one soldier who told him that he was a Christian. The man volunteered to go along and provide whatever protection he could. With his commander's leave, Winfried returned with this Good Samaritan soldier to the compound. The volunteers had continued, in the meantime, to dismantle the equipment and pack it to the best of their ability. Winfried guided them in the completion of the task. All of the containers were packed and loaded onto the truck by day's end. In spite of the soldiers' claims, the compound had not been overrun. It had not even come under attack.

Some of the local crew arranged to stay and guard the truck again through the night. Winfried and Gaby would return in the pre-dawn hours to drive the truck out of the city. The accompanying soldier promised that he would be able to provide other soldiers to escort them, as long as they traveled in the hours before the curfew was lifted.

Winfried arrived back at his hotel. He returned to his room, expecting to find his wife and children. Instead, he opened the door to a darkened and silent room. Suddenly, his worst fears leaped to life. He turned on the lights. All of their belongings had vanished along with Gaby and the children. He raced down the stairs to the lobby and was met by the manager.

"The soldiers took your wife and children," he said. "They will be safer at the barracks."

"Did the mob come here?"

"No, but they found out that this was where you stayed. I needed to assure them that you had gone, and I called the soldiers for help. Otherwise, my hotel might be a pile of ashes right now, and your family killed."

Winfried thanked him for the information and raced across town to the soldiers' barracks. There, to his great relief, he found Gaby and the children, just as he had been told.

The next morning, they drove to the compound at 4:30. A military vehicle with a few soldiers inside led the way. The gates were unlocked, and Winfried silently embraced his local crew leaders. Then he climbed into the cab of the big eighteen-wheeler, and the engine roared to life. He followed the military vehicle into the streets, as Gaby followed him driving the Land Rover.

The blood red trailer bearing Jesus' name began its journey through the smoke and debris of Kano. To their right and left as they passed, the Wentlands saw dead bodies in the streets. Three hundred had been killed. They were forced to maneuver among burned police and military vehicles along the way. The smoking remains of churches, businesses, and petrol stations obscured every turn.

In spite of the "shoot on site" curfew, crowds of zealots could be seen roaming the streets looking for them. Apparently the curfew had been overwhelmed by the sheer number of people willing to violate it. The soldiers were too afraid to try to enforce it. But to Winfried, it was as if the crowds had been made blind.

No one cried out with recognition at the big truck bearing Jesus' name in giant letters. Or, if they did recognize it, like the lions in the den with Daniel, their mouths had been miraculously shut.

They came to a military roadblock. After a few words, the barriers were lifted. They came to another and another with the same results. Every few blocks they found a barricade. They traveled on and on like people for whom the rough way had been made smooth.

In the outer areas of the city they passed through civilian roadblocks. No police or military presence could be detected here. They wondered as they passed, who was in charge. Some of the roadblocks had been erected in Muslim neighborhoods, others in Christian neighborhoods. In all cases, the roadblocks came down and they were allowed to move on. This seemed beyond the range of normal reality.

In retrospect, a notorious incident recorded by the television news media in Los Angeles sheds a sobering light on this passage by the Wentland family. After the Rodney King trial in 1992, the streets of Los Angeles erupted in rioting similar to that in Kano. As helicopters circled overhead, recording the horrible scene for millions of viewers around the world, a truck driver named Reginald Denny was dragged from his eighteen-wheeler and savagely attacked in the street, leaving him with severe head injuries.

Anyone who remembers the vivid television images of the Reginald Denny attack can never forget its sickening force. Many could not look at it all the way through. That kind of viciousness was more likely to be visited upon Winfried and Gaby in Kano than upon Reginald Denny in Los Angeles. I say this because in Kano there were no helicopters circling overhead to remind the rioters that someone was watching.

But Someone was watching. Speaking to each other on walkie-talkies, Winfried and Gaby praised the Lord as they passed safely and easily through block after block of riot-torn neighborhoods. To them it seemed as if the waters of the Red Sea were parting so they could pass through on dry ground.

At the city limits, the military escort vanished, leaving them to travel the seven-hundred-mile road ahead on their own. Soon the big truck and its Jesus trailer was on the open road. Many Muslim cities lay ahead, with news of the Kano riots on everyone's lips. But Winfried and Gaby had gained a confidence to go with their supernatural peace. They believed the trip would continue as it had begun. They were traveling in Jesus' name. They passed through Zaria, Kaduna, Ilorin, and dozens of smaller Muslim dominated communities without a single challenge.

When they arrived back home in Lagos, on the Gulf of Guinea, they were received by an emotional staff that had assumed they were dead. Seeing them arrive, with the children and all of the equipment rescued, a huge celebration erupted.

No one was happier or more relieved than I was when at last I spoke with Winfried by telephone. It was only then that I learned the details of their escape. I privately thanked God that what He had in mind for them was nothing less than a miraculous escape.

In the history of Christ for all Nations, Kano became our greatest setback. Reinhard Bonnke was declared persona non grata in Nigeria, the most populated nation in all of Africa. The rumor mill blamed us, though an extensive report assembled by the local governor exonerated us from all blame for the outbreak of violence. Still, for many people, perception is reality. Bonnke had brought violence to Kano. Did he truly serve the Prince of Peace?

If a public relations firm had produced these results, they would have been fired and branded incompetent. Our tremendous momentum in Nigeria was stopped in its tracks. For many years, it appeared that Satan had won the day in Kano. Jesus had been forced into retreat.

Aren't we glad that God has no public relations firm? He does not see as man sees, and He carries the trump card of the Universe, omnipotence.

How could any of us have known that the bloody events in Kano would catapult our name to the stars in Nigeria? How could anyone have guessed that the eight long years of our banishment would build an irresistible appetite among the people for our return? Who would have anticipated that through the violence of Kano, God was able to build a platform that in the year 2000 would gather 1,600,000 living souls to hear the Gospel in a single meeting? And that, on that day, 1,093,000 of those would register decisions for Christ? Or, that 3,450,000 would accept Jesus in six days of preaching?

The Kano seed is still bearing fruit, and not only in Nigeria. We have documented more than 34 million salvations worldwide in the last three and a half years. By the time you read this book, that number will be totally out of date. Stay tuned.

As we follow Christ we are brought to defining moments
in our faith. Many of us were brought to that threshold
in the streets of Kano. It is a mistake to think that some
of us chose live while others bravely chose to face death.
We all simply chose Him.
And He is Life Eternal.

What you would like to do for money — in terms of varieties to top prizes

A story I read last week — a book given me — a German novelist to oppose R. B. — his team had planned a crusade — when no news only... they had not been heard — Job is done — a team of 6 actors — & said — that 30 or sixty'ch even — each of these stables — ... here of the largest —

— "you'll be a person."
120 years
Past forward — you — when it stops given

But save

CHAPTER
EIGHT

Wow
p121

CRUEL AND UNUSUAL

On August 26, 2001, I preached at the Tata Raphael Grounds in Kinshasa, Zaire. At the close of the sermon, one of my team members said to me, "Reinhard, before you leave, there is someone you should meet." He told me this as he escorted me to the stairs at the back of the stage. As usual, I was drenched in sweat from open-air preaching in the tropics. My blood was pounding. I was still a bit out of breath.

"Who might that be?" I asked.

"A local pastor. He is from one of the churches sponsoring the crusade."

"Why haven't I already met him? We had a Fire Conference for local pastors."

"There were too many. He could not get to you. Besides, at first we didn't know who he was. He's someone special."

We reached an area that had been cordoned off for private meetings. Even in the backstage area at our crusades, crowd control is still essential. We entered the area, and there I saw a small group of my team members standing with a fine looking African pastor.

I knew instantly that I had seen the man before, but I could not recall the incident. He was familiar, but different than I remembered. His eyes were large, brown, and shining with a brilliant light. His smile looked like the full keyboard of my old piano-accordion. Except that his keyboard had one gold key, a large gold tooth shining in the front. He wore a well-pressed, maroon, double-breasted suit with a silk maroon-and-gold tie. He was trembling to see me, and yet still, I could not recall our former meeting.

He could not contain himself any longer. He rushed across the distance between us and threw himself to the ground, wrapping his arms tightly around my legs. He kissed my feet and wept with a loud voice. Gone was his appearance of dignity. He could not care anymore.

"Bonnke," he cried, "I am here because of you. You saved my life. You saved my life."

"Who are you, man?"

I reached down and took his arms, freeing my legs from his grasp. "Stand up here and let me look at you again."

He brought himself up and looked at me, tears streaming from his wonderful brown eyes. He said one word to me, and then I knew him.

"Bukavu."

"Richard," I whispered. "You are Richard?"

My memory rushed back. Twelve years ago I had seen him. I could not believe the change.

"Richard," I said, "the last time I saw you, there was no gold tooth, just an empty socket. You could not speak English, and you were filthy. You stank, excuse me, like an outdoor toilet."

I took his arms and pushed up the sleeves of his fine maroon suit coat and saw the evidence I remembered most. Yes, this was the same man. And now tears spilled from my eyes. I embraced him.

"Richard, what God has done for you! What God has done!"

Where can I begin with the story of Richard? It is so special I fear that I will not do it justice. But I must try. I last saw him in Bukavu, in the extreme eastern borderland of the Congo. Yes, it was Bukavu, 1989. How did we ever get there, to that far-off city? Our journey had started, as I recall, with a scouting report. One of our trucks sank in a river in the Congo. I don't remember which river it was after thirty years of crusades. Nor do I recall the exact year. Anyway, grand old Congo, known today as Zaire, is the most legendary country of Africa. It provided the backdrop for Joseph Conrad's classic story, "Heart of Darkness." Missionaries have told tales of the Congo since the days of Stanley and Livingston. It is a vast land, three times larger than the state of Texas, and it has plenty of rivers big enough to swallow a truck.

I remember that the truck was loaded with gear for a crusade. It rolled onto a ferry and began the crossing. The rainy season had come early. In the middle of the river the ferry began to take on water, and down it went – with our driver inside. He managed to get a window open and swim to the surface of the torrent. He stroked for shore praying for an absence of crocodiles. Just another day on the road to a blood-washed Africa.

Because of incidents like this one, we decided to send out scouting teams. They would create customized road maps for our crusade convoy to use later. When our team traveled to any particular city, they would take advantage of the scouting maps to avoid similar hazards.

Our scouts traveled in Land Rovers equipped with chain saws for clearing fallen trees. And since there are no "Mr. Goodwrench" signs on the fix-it shops out there, they carried every conceivable tool for fixing mechanical trouble on the African back roads. Our scouts are a special breed of problem solvers, and they could tell you stories to fill a book many times larger than this one, believe me.

When they travel, they investigate more than just road conditions. They check out the potential areas in the city for us to set up our crusade platform. They log information about power, water, sewer, local police, crowd control, and any other details that could benefit our planning team. There are a thousand ways to go wrong when conducting an African crusade, and over the years we have found them all. We simply try not to repeat our mistakes. We have learned much, and our scouts are some of the most experienced and fascinating members of our team. They have saved us untold misery, and we have not sunk another truck in another river.

In the late 1980s, a scouting team searched the back roads of the far eastern Congo. As they came near to the border with Rwanda, they came across a city that was not on our list of potential crusade sites. Our planners had simply overlooked it. It was called Bukavu, and it had nearly a half-million citizens who had never seen an evangelistic crusade. Furthermore, the scouting team had confirmed that the roads to the city were passable in the summer. Very excitedly, Stephen Mutua, a team worker called me at our headquarters in Germany.

"Nobody comes here to Bukavu, Reinhard," he said. "We will see tremendous results. It will be glorious."

Nothing makes my heart beat faster than preaching the Gospel where no one else wants to go. This began with my first assignment in the "Gospel-hardened" land of Lesotho in 1969.

"Begin planning a crusade in Bukavu," I ordered. "Stephen, you will be in charge."

The meeting was scheduled. In July of 1989, I flew there to preach. My team met me and escorted me to the hotel where I would be staying. The next day, as I do in every crusade, I asked to be driven around the city. Stephen had been there for months preparing this event, and I wanted him to show me the people I would be preaching to. I wanted to hear from him all that he had learned about the history and lore of Bukavu. We took a local interpreter along. He provided me with a way to interview people in the marketplaces and neighborhoods as we passed through.

At one point in the tour we came to a prison. It was simply a cage for humans, actually, near the edge of the city. There were no cells, just a large brick room with a prison yard attached, surrounded by bars and razor wire. Many of the prisoners were in the yard, taking sunshine, or exercising in the open air. A crowd of people stood around the bars of the yard. Stephen stopped the car and turned off the engine.

"There is a story here, Reinhard," he said.

"What are those people doing outside of the prison yard?" I asked.

"Those are the prisoners' family members. If they don't feed the men, they will die of starvation. The government makes no provision for feeding men they intend to kill."

"All these prisoners will die?"

"All of the ones you see in shackles are condemned to die."

I could see a number of men walking around dragging heavy chains shackled to their arms and legs.

Stephen sighed heavily. "Every month, a hangman comes from Kinshasa. Do you see that tree there?"

Indeed, outside the prison yard was a large tree with large spreading branches.

"Each month," Stephen went on, "the condemned men are all brought out to the tree. A rope is thrown over the big branch with a hangman's noose tied to the end. The people of the city are invited to watch, and many do. For some, it is the local horror show. The hangman earns his living the old fashioned way. There is no scaffold. It is not a merciful hanging like in the old western movies, where there is a long drop to break the neck. Each condemned man in this prison must move forward, one by one, as the noose is placed around his neck. Then the hangman uses the trunk of the tree for leverage to lift the man up, and he ties the rope off until the kicking and choking stops. Then he lets the body down and goes to the next man."

"Have you seen this?"

"I have seen it."

"Can you imagine being one of the condemned, forced to watch what is in store for you?"

"That is not all. When the man is cut down, the hangman hacks off his hands and feet with an axe so that the shackles can be removed. Unless the family comes to claim it, the body is tossed onto a cart, and dumped in an unmarked grave."

"Why doesn't the hangman simply unlock the shackles? Why go to the extreme of cutting off the hands and feet?"

"Because there is no lock. When a condemned man is brought here, he is taken to a blacksmith shed over there. His shackles are welded shut on his arms and legs."

"That cannot be properly done. How do they do that without burning the flesh?"

"The men receive horrible burns. It is part of the punishment. They are considered to be dead already, and no one cares to take care of them. Some have actually died of burn infections before they can be hung. The empty shackles taken from a dead man are opened up with a cutting torch and prepared for the next condemned man. And on it goes. Welcome to Bukavu."

I had seen this in other places. Once again, I realized that an African prison was a place to be feared. Unlike prisons in western nations, in this remote part of the world, a prisoner's rights were unheard of. There was little public scrutiny of the justice system. All major political leaders were appointed, not elected. The people in power were expected to dominate the population by fear and intimidation. I had met many leaders in Africa who used their prison system to get rid of potential rivals and political enemies. Justice was often miscarried. It reminded me of what prison life must have been like in the biblical days of Paul and Silas.

"Here is the good news," Stephen offered. "I've been visiting here, and several of the condemned men have accepted Jesus. I've been having a Bible study with them for several weeks now."

"Praise God, Stephen," I said. "I want to meet them. Take me inside to meet my brothers in the Lord."

We got out of the car. Immediately, a strange sound came to my ears. It was the rhythmic jangle of chains mingled with the chant of male African voices.

"Hear that?" Stephen asked, with a knowing smile. "Those are your brothers."

"My brothers? What are they doing?"

"They are singing songs of praise to Jesus. Songs we taught them. They are using the only musical instruments they have."

"Their chains," I whispered, with realization. I stood there and listened, and as I did, I sensed Someone Else listening with me. As the sound of that wonderful haunting chant rose in the humid air, I sensed a door standing open, straight into the throne room of God. I could almost see the great archangels at the Portal of Heaven standing to receive this sacrifice of praise. My spirit flew like a bird from a cage. Something wonderful was about to happen.

Meanwhile, Stephen approached the guards, explaining who I was. They apparently already knew Stephen. We were allowed inside. The song continued.

I was appalled by the conditions in the cell. The men slept on filthy mattresses scattered about on the floor of that large cement block room. The place was crawling with vermin. Buckets of sewage were gathered to one side. Clouds of flies swarmed over them. In the stifling heat, none of us could escape the stench. And the song, that wonderful chant of praise, continued to rise to the Lord with the jangle of chains.

We went out into the yard. Immediately, several men in their shackles gathered around us. Stephen spoke through the interpreter, explaining who I was. I greeted them briefly, but I was looking for the singing men.

I saw them, sitting in a circle, about thirty in all. They were singing and swaying to the music. Their leader was a man of average build with a big smile and a missing front tooth. He rattled his chains with a real flourish, like a choir leader in a big church. If I had truly seen with the eyes of the Spirit, I might have seen him wearing a fine maroon suit.

The minute I saw him, the Holy Spirit spoke to me, *Tell that man he will be set free.*

Lord, pardon me, but it would cruel and unusual to say anything if I heard You wrongly just now. Please, say it again. More slowly this time.

Tell that man he will be set free.

We were introduced to the group of condemned men. I greeted the brothers who had accepted the Lord in the name of Jesus. I gave the whole group a salvation sermon through the interpreter. A few of them responded, accepting Jesus for the first time. I then encouraged them in the Lord. Then I turned to Stephen.

"Tell that man who was leading the singing that I would like to speak to him in private."

Stephen went to the man, explaining my request. He brought him to me, with the interpreter. We walked to a vacant area in the yard.

"Reinhard," Stephen said, "this man's name is Richard."

It was an honor to shake his shackled hand. "Tell Richard that the Lord has spoken to me today. The Lord says that he will be set free."

The interpreter hesitated.

I nodded. "Repeat my words exactly," I said.

He cleared his throat and spoke to the man in his native tongue. The man reacted, looking away toward the hanging tree. When he looked back at me, his eyes had filled with tears. He spoke through the interpreter.

"Three times I have waited in line. Three times the hangman has become too tired to hang me. The last time he was here, I was the next man to die. The hangman glared at me like he wanted to see me dead. Then he threw up his hands and went home."

"Jesus preserves you, Richard," I said. "And now He says you will be set free."

Richard listened. I could tell that he was still too afraid to reach out and take my word for it. Hope can be most cruel to a condemned man waiting to hang. A man who has seen the end of his life played out for him so graphically, time after time. A man who wears shackles welded to his arms and legs, shackles that he has seen removed only one way.

"What is your crime, Richard? What are you guilty of?"

"Murder."

"You do not look like a murderer. Who did you kill?"

He named the man.

"How did it happen?"

"We were in a bar, and a fight started."

"Did you start the fight?"

"I did not. But I did kill the man."

"Richard, if what you say is true, we do not call that murder. It is called self-defense. Did you have a lawyer?"

Richard paused for a long time. He looked away at the tree again, and said nothing.

Then the interpreter spoke.

"If the man you kill in self-defense is from a wealthy family, Reverend Bonnke, there are many in Bukavu willing to swear testimony for money."

We left the prison and I never saw Richard again. I preached for several days in the soccer stadium to standing-room-only crowds of 90,000. This created a huge stir in the area. Bukavu had never seen crowds like these in its history. Nearly everyone in the region attended at least one of the meetings. The number of salvations registered exceeded all that we had hoped and prayed for. We were ecstatic.

As I prepared to leave, I asked Stephen Mutua to arrange one more meeting for me. I named a leading local politician. I will not here name the man, nor his office, because of the nature of the story that follows.

When we arrived at the politician's mansion we were ushered into a waiting area. We were kept waiting for a long time. Waiting to see powerful people in Africa is something that I have learned that I must do. Finally, a secretary emerged from the inner sanctum, and told us that the politician I wished to see was not available.

Now, if this is true, I thought, they might have told us earlier, in time to spare us this trip. Either it is a lie, or they have decided the great evangelist must prove his Christianity by demonstrating nearly infinite patience in the waiting room.

The politician was on a trip to Kinshasa, we were told. Instead of seeing him, we would be allowed to meet briefly with his wife. She would relay everything to her husband after we had gone.

After more waiting, a tall woman entered the room. She was dressed in finery and beautiful fabrics. I thought she carried herself with the imperial dignity of the Queen of Sheba. When she had made her entrance, an interpreter was provided, and I was able, at last, to speak to her.

After formalities, I told her why I had asked to see her husband. I had come to plead for the release of a condemned man in Bukavu prison, a man named Richard. I described him to her, and I recited his story of the crime for which he was sentenced to die. I suggested to her that a competent lawyer would surely have made a case for self defense. At least a good lawyer would have found a way to avoid the death penalty for Richard. Then I told her of Richard's conversion, and of the way he led the singing among the condemned men in the prison.

She listened carefully to all that I said. Then she stood and excused herself. She said that she would see about what could be done, but condemned prisoners were never released from Bukavu prison once the courts had spoken.

After another long time of waiting, she returned. She asked that all of the other guests be removed from the room. At last it was just the two of us. She stood before me, very close.

"Reverend Bonnke," she said, quietly. "You are a very powerful man from Germany. Your organization is large, and your following is wide. You want my husband to do something for you. I would like you to do something for me. Do you understand?"

"Certainly," I said, "I will do whatever I can."

"Do you have children, Reverend Bonnke?"

133

"Yes, I do."

"I have two children preparing to attend the university. Here, we have only the National University of Zaire." She shrugged, as if I would understand her problem. "It is not the educational excellence that you would want for your children, I am sure. And yet, my children have not been able to get the necessary scholarships to the schools we would choose abroad. I would like you to provide those scholarships, Reverend Bonnke. Will you do that for me?"

I was saddened, though not truly surprised. In a land where money could buy a death sentence, surely a bribe could obtain freedom.

"I am sorry," I said, "but this, I cannot do. I am a man of God. I will not strike a bargain to obtain justice of any kind. My answer to you must be no."

The woman instantly whirled to leave the room. I feared greatly for Richard. As she reached for the door, I nearly shouted her name. She stopped and looked back at me for one moment. I pointed my finger at her.

"God has told me that Richard will be released. God has spoken. Do not stand in His way."

She left the room, shutting the door behind her with force. My meeting was over.

"Oh, Lord," I prayed, "save Richard by Your mighty power, not by the power of bribes and treachery."

I must confess, I left Bukavu with a heavy heart. I feared that I had left Richard as I had found him, a dead man walking. My one hope was that the politician's wife feared God in some corner of her heart, and that the Holy Spirit would cause my words to find their mark.

Two years passed. I was in Germany when someone reported to me that Richard had been set free. I shouted with joy to hear of it. To this day, I do not know what happened, or what triggered his release. I only know that all the glory belongs to Our Father in Heaven.

Meanwhile, Richard began a new life as a free man in Bukavu. He told the pastor of the local church where he attended that he wanted to go to Bible college in Kenya. He wanted to become a pastor, and he was determined to learn to speak English. When the word of this got back to me – well, that was one scholarship I was more than willing to provide. Christ for all Nations paid for Richard's expenses through Bible college. Years later, I heard the news of his ordination. I sent him my best wishes and congratulations, and that seemed a fitting end to it.

Twelve years later, in August of 2001, he stood before me in Kinshasa, a sponsoring pastor for a Christ for all Nations Crusade. He was wearing his maroon double-breasted suit, speaking good English, his gold tooth shining, his eyes bright with the joy of the Lord.

We embraced again. I can tell you, this evangelist slept so very well that night.

❧

Two long years of waiting passed in this story before
I learned about its happy ending. How did I handle it
in the meantime? I have learned that when we speak the
words that God has whispered in our hearts, we don't
have to handle it – He does. The Scripture says that He
watches over His word to perform it.
We can rest easy.

CHAPTER NINE

A THEOLOGY TOO SMALL

For seven years after leaving Lesotho I conducted crusades in South Africa, Botswana, Swaziland, Zimbabwe, and Zambia. We saw hundreds of thousands come to the Lord, and many notable miracles of healing. God had spoken that our ministry would extend beyond the borders of Africa. So, I had named our organization, Christ for all Nations.

In 1980, I ventured to hold a campaign in Birmingham, England. This was my first crusade outside of Africa. Then, early in 1983, another invitation came to hold a crusade in the city of Perth, on the sunny west coast of Australia. Our friends in that city had acquired the use of the 8,000-seat Entertainment Center. And so we came there.

The first night the hall was packed. The local Channel 4 news team arrived to make a story for their late edition. As I came onto the stage, I began a conversation with the Lord. "What will you do here tonight, Lord?" My eyes were drawn to the far right side of the auditorium where a lady in a blue dress sat in a wheelchair. The Lord said to me, "*Tonight I will heal that woman in the blue dress.*" Now, this was not something I heard acoustically. It was a message in my heart. I accepted it.

Early in the meeting, I got up to greet the people. I took the microphone and announced, with great excitement, "Today a great miracle is going to happen here in Perth, Australia. Right in this entertainment center." I pointed to the woman in the blue dress, "That woman over there is going to be healed, and she is coming out of her wheelchair." The Channel 4 news team took eager notice of it, for better or worse.

When I made this announcement, I hoped to stir up an expectation in the crowd. I had learned that this can help build an atmosphere of faith. Until this day in Perth, I had found that unless faith was present, miracles did not happen. I based this on my own experience, as well as on Scripture.

In the Gospels of Matthew and Mark, we read that Jesus' miracle-working power was limited by the unbelief of the people in Nazareth. Certainly, if a lack of faith can limit Jesus' power to do miracles, it can limit mine. At other times, we find Jesus saying to people who were healed, "Your faith has made you whole." If Jesus credited miracles of healing to the faith of the sick person, so must I. This was my theology of faith in a nutshell. In this case, I learned that God likes to crack theological nutshells.

As I made my bold announcement about God healing the woman, it did not seem to build an atmosphere of faith in the room. In fact, the opposite happened. The woman did not receive my announcement as good news. She ducked her head under her arms and tried to hide herself. I must have sounded to those people like an insensitive South African preacher who had presumed upon a poor woman's illness. It appeared that she wanted to drop through a hole in the floor. For a moment, so did I. The crowd did not respond positively. The atmosphere grew cool, and I sat down.

What I did not know was that this woman had merely come as an invited guest. She was not religious at all. She had no knowledge or expectation of healing. Of course, neither did I know her condition. I was relying only on what I had heard from the Lord in my spirit. It turns out the woman had a degenerative disease called "brittle bone" disease. To stand up would cause her bones to crack. The doctors had said she would never walk again.

As I waited for the time for preaching, I said within myself, *"Oh Lord, she doesn't have faith. How's this going to work?"*

In a moment the Holy Spirit spoke back to me, *"Today it's not her faith, it's your faith. You are going to see a great miracle."*

This idea was too big for my theology-in-a-nutshell. She didn't have faith, but my faith was enough for her miracle? Immediately, my mind raced through the Scriptures. Could I find an example in the New Testament that would demonstrate that Jesus healed someone based on the faith of another?

Suddenly it came to me: the story of the paralyzed man who was let down through the roof to Jesus. In the story, the man shows no faith of his own. His friends take him to Jesus. They cannot get into the house where He is teaching, but they are so sure of Jesus' power to heal that they remove the roofing material, and let the man down next to the Lord inside the house. The Bible says that when Jesus saw their faith, he forgave the man's sins and healed his body. This was clearly a gift of faith from the man's friends to him through Jesus. The story is found in the second chapter of Mark. Who was I to say it couldn't be done that way in Perth, Australia in 1983?

Now I had my text for the evening. When I got up to preach, I preached to myself as much as to anyone else. I built up my own faith by this Bible story so that when the time came to pray for the woman, I would not expect her faith to be present.

At the end of the sermon, I announced that I would now pray for the woman in the wheelchair, as I had promised. On the platform with me was a pastor friend from South Africa. He whispered, "Reinhard, you're on your own now." By this he meant that he had seen the woman's lack of faith, and was not going to share my embarrassment.

I went with the voice of the Spirit. I came down from the platform and walked to the wheelchair. The TV crew got in position to record the event.

"What is your name?" I asked.

"I am Mrs. McKelt."

"Mrs. McKelt, God has told me that you are going to be healed today."

As I prepared to lay my hands on her I felt a tap on my shoulder. It was my South African friend. "One shall chase a thousand," he whispered, "but two can chase ten thousand." He was speaking now of joining his faith with mine in this prayer. I would have prayed without him, but I was glad to see him there.

I laid my hands on her head and commanded, "In the name of Jesus, get up and walk!"

Slowly, unsteadily, she stood to her feet. The people seemed to be holding their breath. Channel 4 was filming away.

"Now walk," I said.

She began to walk like Frankenstein – clump, clump, clump, across the floor. She moved like she was wearing lead boots.

"Run in Jesus' name!" I shouted. "Run!"

Suddenly, she took off like a shot. She began running, and screaming, and laughing, and jumping. She acted like a person who has just received an extreme makeover from the Creator of the Universe, pain free, in ten seconds flat.

News 4 ran the story. The next day they did a follow up, taking their camera to her house. When she answered the door the camera revealed her wheelchair folded up in a corner of the entryway. Needless to say, our meetings in Perth were standing room only from that point on.

Years later, Mrs. McKelt attended a Christ for all Nations partners banquet in Perth. She came to show me that she was completely healed. No more broken bones. She was a child of God set free. For me she was another example of God's love and amazing grace. I just praise Him.

Through Mrs. McKelt, I learned to be careful about putting God in a theological box. But even when I do, I know that I can be made free by listening to and obeying the voice of His Spirit. Today, when I pray for someone and that person is not healed, I do not blame him or her in my mind for a lack of faith.

The longer I live the less I pretend to know about the mind of God. I do not know why some are healed when others are not. I only know that sometimes it is the gift of someone else's faith that can make a person whole.

CHAPTER
TEN

A PROMISE TO COUNT ON

All day long, Sulamith Mörtzschke watched little children growing up. She was a kindergarten teacher. She loved her work, yet it brought her pain because she wanted a child of her own so badly.

Her husband, a young lawyer near Frankfurt, was just starting his practice. On weekends he served as worship leader at their church. He was a fine and respected man, and she wanted to please him more than anyone she had ever known. They both felt called to be godly parents, bringing up children to serve the Lord. But after five years of trying to conceive, she knew that something was wrong.

Sulamith began to blame herself. She felt that her inability to conceive somehow made her less of a woman. In the depths of her heart, she sensed that her husband could have done better if he had picked another mate. Every woman she met seemed a better candidate.

Each day at kindergarten, a painful drama was repeated again and again as mothers came to pick up their children. A toddler would suddenly cry out his or her mother's name and rush to the door for a wild embrace. Sulamith could hardly bear to watch anymore, fearing that she would never hear that sound from her own child, nor know that bond of true motherhood. This pain nagged her so much that she could hardly meet the gaze of the mothers she served. She felt inferior and unworthy of their esteem.

In desperation, she and her husband visited their family doctor. After many consultations with no success, he referred them to the Child Wish Center. This was the clinic of last resort in the region of Germany where they lived. All of the latest reproductive techniques were in use there every day. The combined knowledge of all the medical specialties that could help them was available for a price. And the price was high.

A series of comprehensive tests was started. They began with extensive interviews. The staff asked many personal questions about their family background and their personal lives. Then the medical tests were done. Was it a malfunction in her ovaries? Or could it be his sperm count? The doctors used every method available to determine who was at fault. Some of the tests were humiliating for both of them. At times they felt like lab rats. When they went home from the clinic they felt saddened. It seemed wrong to be investigating a gift from God with such intrusive methods. And yet, they didn't know what else to do.

At this very time, I had planned a Christ for all Nations Fire Conference in Böblingen, Germany. Their church cooperated with our ministry in this effort. I was so excited. It was 1999, and we were celebrating twenty-five years of organized evangelistic effort. The partners that lived in the area of Böblingen had been among the very first to support me as we had begun. Now, I could celebrate our long association by bringing this twenty-fifth anniversary conference to their city.

As in all such conferences, I am focused on inspiring every believer to his or her calling as a witness for Jesus Christ. Not only do I preach, but I invite special speakers who I feel can make a clear challenge on this point. On the final night, evangelist Steve Hill spoke. His sermon hit the mark. It was a fitting end to a wonderful conference of workshops and seminars.

In the audience that night, Sulamith and her husband were deeply touched. In their hearts they made new commitments to witness for Jesus. As they returned to their everyday lives, they would seek to preach the Gospel to everyone the Lord brought across their path.

I came to the podium to close the meeting in prayer. I asked the audience to bow their heads, and I began to pray God's blessing and power into the lives of all of those present. I began to lift up the coming year of crusades. Our planning committee had called it "The Millennium Harvest." I believed that during that special year of 2000, God would do great things through us, with a record number of souls plundered from Hell and registered in Heaven. All of these thoughts were pouring from me in prayer like a fountain of fresh spring water.

As I prayed at the podium, however, Sulamith became overwhelmed with a feeling of desperation. Nothing meant more to her as a soul winner than guiding the growth of her own child, dedicated to God from her womb. She began to plead with God. "Dear Lord, please speak to Reinhard about our need. Please let him say something about our desire for a baby."

At the podium, I suddenly stopped. It was abrupt. The Spirit was tapping at the door of my heart. My ministry director, Peter van den Berg, and others who were with me on the platform, still remember this moment.

"I feel that I should not go on," I said, "until I have prayed for the sick. I will now pray for the sick before we leave this place."

145

As I began to pray, the Spirit pressed these words into my heart and mind. I spoke them aloud, "Someone here has an intense desire to have a child. Count from this day, nine months, and you shall have a baby." I felt it so strongly, I said it again, "count from this day, nine months, and you shall have a baby."

Meanwhile, Sulamith could hardly contain herself. *Could these words be for me, Lord?*

The meeting ended and I heard nothing to confirm that I had heard from the Lord in this wonderful promise for a baby to be born. The delegates filtered out of the hall, returning to their homes.

That night Sulamith talked about it with her husband in the car as he drove. She told him how she had secretly prayed that God would speak to me as I had delivered the closing prayer. Her faith had been ignited as I had stopped to address that very thing. This promise simply had to be for them, she believed.

Her husband struggled to raise his hopes to believe that God had interrupted this great meeting just to deliver a message to them. But he could not deny that I had spoken those amazing words. He talked with his wife about it all the way home, deciding to try to reach out and embrace this nine-month prophecy for themselves. If God had spoken to them through my words, they decided, it would simply come to pass.

Ten days after the conference their telephone rang. A staff member from the Child Wish Center called with bad news. The medical experts at the clinic had examined all of the data from their fertility tests and had reached a conclusion: there was no hope for them to ever conceive a child. The clinic did not recommend that anything more be done. The doctors had determined that artificial fertilization would not work in their case. Not even surgery would make a difference. The staff member said that the doctors had suggested that they turn their full attention toward adopting a child. It was their only hope.

Sulamith was stunned. All of her hopes, lifted so high by my words at the conference, came crashing down like a shattered crystal goblet. The Lord had told her to count nine months. The doctors were telling her to count nothing at all.

Feelings of inferiority descended like a dark cloud. She had suspected that she was a failure as a woman, now she had confirmation. The ache of never bearing a child as a biological mother returned with a vengeance. She could not think about adoption-not just now. She could hear only the silence of the nursery she had built in her mind for the child she would never hold.

As she placed the phone down she flushed with a burst of anger. After all they had invested to learn the truth from the Child Wish Center, how could such sensitive and devastating news be delivered in an impersonal phone call? The insult of this added an even greater level of pain to her sense of injury.

Days later, a letter arrived from the clinic confirming everything she had heard in the phone call. As she shared it with her husband, they both knew that their earlier decision to accept God's word to them had taken on added weight. In black and white, they now knew how impossible it would be for them to conceive by any natural means. Their faith was shaken, but also strengthened in a strange way. If they would have a child, only God could make it happen.

Sulamith returned to her kindergarten. She watched other people's children play. She helped them learn about God and His love for them. She poured herself into helping these little ones grow in the nurture and admonition of the Lord. All the while, her heart fluttered between the sudden hope of God's promise at the Fire Conference and the cruel disappointment that had come from the doctor's report. Each day she reached out anew to believe for the impossible. And each day she would wonder if God had spoken to another woman – not her – through Reinhard Bonnke's prophecy at the Fire Conference. Meanwhile, her husband poured himself into his work, leaving little time to think or talk about it.

Seven weeks passed. Sulamith sensed that something was different in her. At first she dared not say anything, but her body was definitely going through changes. At last she shared these new feelings with her husband. Immediately, he scheduled a trip to the doctor.

The doctor did his testing and could not believe the results. Sulamith was seven weeks pregnant. Impossible!

Ten weeks after the conference, I received an email telling me that a pregnancy had resulted from the promise spoken at the Fire Conference. The mother and baby tested normal and healthy, and the due date was February 23, 2000 – exactly nine months from the day God had declared it.

Today, the Mörtzschkes are raising two healthy children in the fear and admonition of the Lord. One child attends kindergarten where his mother is a teacher. Sulamith has received the desires of her heart.

I tell you by the same Spirit that whispered to my heart in Böblingen that night, God has good plans for you. Count on it.

We sometimes think of doctors as enemies of faith. This
is only true if we allow it to be true. God is Lord over
medicine, too. He can use doctors to play their role,
wittingly or unwittingly, in His divine purpose.

CHAPTER
ELEVEN

THE SILENT SCREAM

I play a small, supporting role in this wonderful love story. So, I will step aside and tell it as David and Rita tell it. David Attah had been raised in a Muslim home in Nigeria. He was of average height, trim of build, and he had a sensitive and pleasant face. Wearing wire-rimmed glasses for nearsightedness, he carried himself with the look of a man of gentle intelligence.

Inside, he had hurt for many years. An only child, his mother had died when he was a boy. He had never been wanted by his cold, stern father. Friendships had been few. But he had reached his limit. One day he simply decided to lose his loneliness.

He moved to Makurdi, into a house with a group of students, and enrolled as a communications major at the local branch of the Nigerian State University. He put a smile on his face and a warm greeting in his mouth for everyone he met. Soon he had reached his goal. He was surrounded by friends. He had lost his loneliness.

Nearly four years of diligent study passed. The pain of his past was buried as he enjoyed the companionship he craved. When his friends had trouble, he was there to listen and care. When they had financial trouble, he would dip into his own wallet and make loans. Some were never repaid. He would sometimes turn them into gifts. David liked being a rescuer. With such qualities, he became popular. Students, faculty, even the maintenance crew – everybody loved David Attah.

An evangelist came to town. David attended his meetings with a fellow student named Jonah. He had always believed in God. For David, the big question was, "What kind of God is He?" His Muslim family had taught him that Allah was absolutely sovereign; he planned everything before it happened. The best anyone could do was accept his fate: "Allah wills it." But David had been fated to be a lonely boy, and he had rejected that fate. He was ready to receive the Christian God, who said, "You must be born again." He loved the Christian language of new birth, starting over, and second chances.

The crusade sermon presented a God of love who had died for the sins of the world. All of the harsh Muslim beliefs that he had picked up along the way seemed to fit the personality of his earthly father: unloving, unyielding, uncaring. By contrast, Jesus revealed a heavenly Father of love, who had sent His Son to die for the world. The choice seemed clear. He raised his hand and repeated the sinner's prayer, embracing Christ as his Savior. Now his new life of friends and fellowship would last forever.

Suddenly, everything changed. As he walked to school, a woman sped through an intersection near the campus, striking David down. Police arrived. The woman was arrested and charged with driving under the influence. David knew nothing. He remained unconscious with severe head injuries, broken bones, and possible internal bleeding. An ambulance took him away.

When he opened his eyes again, he was in a hospital room. He heard a familiar voice say, "You've been out for two days." Through blurred vision, he saw that his arms and legs were encased in plaster. His head throbbed, and it was wrapped in bandages. He struggled to remember what had happened to him.

He had been walking to class. Suddenly, everyone was rushing to get away from a speeding car, but someone had blocked his path. He recalled that he seemed to be out of his body in an eerie, silent vacuum. He watched his wire-rimmed glasses fly up into the blue, he saw his body summersault as if in slow motion, then he heard the sickening thud of the car hitting him. Time had slipped out of sync in his mind. Things that should have happened first, happened after; and things happened after, that should have happened first. There had been a flash of light, and then everything had plunged into a darkness lasting forty-eight hours.

Now, he was here in a hospital room. He discerned the shape of Jonah near his bedside. It had been Jonah's familiar voice that he had heard as he awakened. They were roommates, and were scheduled to graduate together. Final exams would begin in a few weeks. From the extent of his injuries, David knew that he would not recover in time to finish school with his friends. His dream of starting a career in communications had been given a huge setback. How could God have chosen this time to decree such an evil fate for him? Perhaps Allah was God after all.

He closed his eyes. Every beat of his heart sent a pulsing ache across his eyelids. It was like an iron anvil had been dropped on his chest. Each breath was labored, and shot fingers of pain through his rib cage. He wanted only to sleep. But he told himself that he must awaken at 3 a.m. so that he could pray. That was the magic hour. From the dimness of childhood he recalled the creed: We believe in what His Messenger told us, that He descends to the near sky before the last third of every night and says: "Who prays to me and I will answer his prayers? Who asks me and I will give him?" As his battered body gave in to sleep, David wondered why Allah asked questions at 3 a.m. Why did he not give answers?

When he awoke again, the sun was high. He had missed his chance to pray. A nurse checked his vital signs. He decided to ask her the extent of his injuries, but as he attempted to form the words, no movement or sound came from his mouth. This alarmed him. He had developed the skill of expressing kindness and gratitude toward those around him, which in turn, made them eager to help him. But the words in his head could not force any movement into his tongue. It was like the connection had been cut.

He thought that the bandage on his head might be too tight across his jaw, restricting his speech. But his arms were held back by the casts so that he could not check it. He struggled to speak to the nurse again. Forget speech – he tried to make a sound, a groan, a moan – nothing happened. The nurse looked at him with sympathy, and left the room. He began to feel strangely disconnected. Fear swept through his mind like a wildfire.

On the bedside stand he saw his Bible. Jonah must have left it for him. The sight of it reminded him that, unlike Allah, the God of the Bible was always ready to hear prayers, twenty-four hours a day. He would not have to awaken at 3 a.m. to impress Him with his devotion. Perhaps he should pray to his heavenly Father after all, praying in the name of Jesus. But what would he pray? Would he pray for protection from harm or accidents? It was a little late for that. Would he pray for healing? He would think about prayer later. For the present, his faith was as battered as his body.

In the months ahead, the hard work of therapy began. During that time, a neurosurgeon from Makurdi General Hospital tested David's speech. He discovered that he still had marvelous language skills and was able to write. But David had totally lost the ability to make his mouth utter, or even whisper, a single word. The doctor consulted the medical journals. He returned to tell David that this was a well-documented disorder resulting from a head injury. It was called *aphasia*. There were many different types of aphasia, but David's type was clearly noted in the literature.

In the weeks of rehabilitation that followed, David gained the use of his right hand. He communicated his thoughts by note pad. The doctors and staff at the hospital developed affection for their bright and sensitive patient. They made special efforts to encourage him. They told him that one day his ability to speak might return just as mysteriously as it had gone. But David found it hard to endure that kind of hope. To him, it seemed totally concocted. He wanted a clear physical diagnosis and a true medical cure. Otherwise, he would rather not hear such patronizing lies.

In the meantime, the hospital bills were real enough. They mounted beyond all reason. Nothing was given freely at Makurdi General. The drugs for pain and the blood thinners ate up 250 naira per day, not including room and board, plus medical testing. Within a few weeks, his money was gone. He was sinking deeply into debt.

The hospital required patients to pay for meals. He could not afford to purchase them anymore. To slow the rising flood of I.O.U.s, he began to ask for scraps and leftovers from his fellow patients. People liked him so much, they actually kept back food for him. He managed to get by on this kind of charity for a while.

Meanwhile, his classmates at the university graduated. They became busy seeking new lives and careers. He had visits from Jonah and other student-friends in the first days after the accident. After spending some hours at his bedside, they grew impatient. The David they had known was quick-witted and full of bright conversation. Now, all of his answers had to be written out, and he seemed to have lost his ability to bounce back. Conversation became hard work. In frustration, Jonah accused him of faking the dumbness. "Why don't you just get over it?" he said, and left the room, never to be seen again.

David decided to sell his belongings to pay his prescription drug bill. He sent someone to collect his things from the house that he had shared with fellow students, but when he arrived, his room was bare. It seems his old friends had stolen everything. Perhaps they had sold his things to pay his overdue rent. Whatever the reason, they had not bothered to share their plans with him. He never saw his university friends again.

This hit him hard. The new life he had made for himself in Makurdi, surrounded by friends, had been a mirage. Perhaps he was fated to be lonely after all, and nothing had ever really changed. Old things did not pass away. All things did not become new. He began to plunge into fits of depression.

With no place to go, no immediate family to welcome him, David stayed in the hospital. Weeks turned into months. One day a national television crew came and filmed a story about him. The local neurosurgeon described his case to the audience. It was broadcast nationwide, and David's name and face was seen across Nigeria. The publicity was used to raise money for the hospital. After that, he became affectionately known as "The Chairman" of the hospital board. The staff and patients treated him as if he owned the place.

But he had no illusions; the hospital owned him, and every penny he would make for the rest of his life. Besides, he had once enjoyed this kind of adulation from his many friends at the university. He knew that those who pledged their devotion today would fail him tomorrow.

One day, the neurosurgeon ordered an MRI (Magnetic Resonance Imaging) scan to be done on David's head. From the results he suggested a surgery could be done to remove some scar tissue at the back of his head that was putting pressure on his brain. He said that this delicate operation might bring positive results for him. No promises, but the very hint of regaining his speech peaked David's desire. He was willing to risk anything for it. He agreed to the surgery. But the political situation in Nigeria went through a sudden upheaval. The doctor fled the country with his family. All plans for David's surgery were abandoned.

Enough was enough. David decided to end the pain. He took advantage of his free access to the pharmacy, stealing a supply of poison. He prepared a lethal dose for himself. If God had fated him for loneliness, debt, failure, and dumbness, he wanted out. He would go see this God face to face and ask Him to give the assignment to someone else.

He sat down and wrote a letter. He thanked the hospital staff for all of their efforts. He made it clear that his death was by his own hand. In the letter, he described the reasons that he would kill himself. "Life is not worth living," he wrote. "I will always be alone. Nothing matters."

He placed the letter inside his Bible, which he laid on the nightstand. Then he lay down. His plan was to wait until the ward was asleep, and then he would take the poison. No one would find him until it was too late.

He felt a strange sense of peace with this decision. The constant turmoil that afflicted his mind day and night, simply ceased. He later realized that the author of death, the enemy of his soul, cooperates with those who decide to help his evil cause.

As he lay there, resolved to suicide, Someone Else had bigger and better plans for him. A beautiful girl with large, kind eyes, walked into his room. At first David thought he was dreaming. She was not a member of the nursing staff. He knew everyone at Makurdi General, and he would have remembered this lovely creature.

"Can I talk with you?" she asked.

Her voice was soft and warm. She spoke with a steady tone that seemed rooted in the very earth beneath her. He wondered, Is this an angel? He stared at her.

"I know you can't speak," she said. "But they tell me that you write very well."

He sat up, and nodded. He took a note pad and wrote, "Who are you?"

She came near and bent down to read his note. He could detect the delicate floral scent of her perfume. It filled his head with the idea that if he had no reason to live for himself, he might go on living for someone else.

"My name is Rita. I am training to be a nurse," she said.

"So, they sent you to practice on me?" he wrote.

"No, I am curious about you. I saw you on television and I wanted to come see you. I have talked to the staff here. They tell me you're depressed." She reached out and picked up David's Bible. "Are you a Christian?"

He nodded.

a sister — in God

"I knew it!" she exclaimed. "So am I." Her smile was full and lovely. She opened his Bible and saw the note he had just written. "May I read this?"

David froze inside. He wasn't sure why he wanted to give her permission to read his suicide note, but in some part of himself he did. He nodded, and then watched as her expression changed to one of alarm.

She looked at him, her brows darkly knit. "You must never, never do this!" she said. "I want you to promise me that you will not do this terrible thing."

David looked away. He could not promise her. He could not promise himself. He shook his head.

She became offended, and spoke sharply. "Do you really believe in God, David?"

He nodded.

"Did God give you life?"

David thought of Allah, and of the Christian God. In either case, the answer was yes. He nodded.

"Then He will not forgive you if you take this precious gift by your own hand." She was pacing back and forth, piercing him with her gaze. "It is not your life to take, David. It is His. You will go to Hell if you murder yourself. And I do not want you to go to Hell."

David wondered if Hell was as lonely as his life. He took his pad and wrote, "My family is gone. My friends have betrayed me. I have lost everything I own. My education has become worthless. I cannot pay my debts. I am alone, and not even God cares."

As Rita read this, she heard a voice speaking in her spirit. "*If you want him to make this promise, you must make a promise to be his friend.*"

Rita spoke slowly, deliberately, "God cares very much about you, David. He sent me to you today. If you will promise me that you will never take your life, I will promise you something in return. It's only fair."

David could not believe she was saying this. He had never once heard anyone make such an intimate proposal to a total stranger. He took his pad and wrote, "How can you promise me anything? You don't know me."

"You don't know me either. If you will promise me that you will not take your life," she said, "then I will promise to stand by you, no matter what. I will be your friend."

"No one can promise that," he wrote.

"This is not a promise to you, David. It is a promise I make to God in my heart. He will help me to keep it. But I will make no promise at all to someone who plans to kill himself. Do you understand me?"

In her words, David heard what he longed most to hear – a pledge of unconditional loyalty. But he could not believe that this beautiful girl, nor anyone, would live up to such a promise. Besides, Rita was of marrying age, and many men would want to have her for a wife. If she married, her husband would never tolerate such a promise to stand by another man.

"Promise me," she said.

He had absolutely nothing to lose. Could it be that God had sent this girl to break him out of his silent prison? He reached out beyond himself, and decided to make her this promise. Taking his pad, he wrote, "I promise you, Rita, not to take my own life."

"Sign your name," she said.

He signed his name.

"Date it," she demanded.

He added the date.

She reached down and took the paper from beneath his hand. Holding it up, she read it again. She carefully folded it and placed it in her purse. Then she took the suicide note from the open Bible.

"I promise God, and you, David," she said, as she tore the note to shreds, "that I will be your true friend from this day on."

The next day, Rita came to his hospital room with a prepared meal. She came the next day and the next. She ran errands for him. She did his laundry. They began long hours of conversation, she talking, he writing his answers. She treasured his wonderful way with words, so she brought three-ringed binders to keep his writings in.

Around the hospital the patients and staff began to joke with David, "Here comes your wife," they would say, whenever Rita approached. David was flattered. He hardly deserved such a wife.

His debts mounted higher. David decided to sue the woman who had hit him with the car. Rita helped him with the months' long legal process. At the end of the trial, a sympathetic jury awarded him 1,000,000 naira in damages. He was happy to think that this would pay his hospital bills, and provide for his continuing drug expenses. As the months passed, however, it became clear that the guilty woman had many ways to avoid paying her fine. Legal appeals and challenges to the verdict abounded, slowing and diverting the payoff. David's emotional state went up and down with the legal fight.

Meanwhile, Rita was accepted to nursing school in Enugu, hundreds of miles away. She promised that she would not neglect him, but would return to Makurdi. In the meantime, she located a local ministry that served widows and orphans. They agreed to take David on as a ministry project while she was away. While studying in Enugu, Rita continued her conversation with him in letters, writing every day as the months of her schooling progressed.

In time, she graduated. Her family was happy and excited for her. They wanted her to seek work in Lagos, or other more attractive locations in Nigeria. She would be accepted anywhere she chose, they told her. Since she spoke English, she might even find a job in America. But she refused to consider an assignment outside of Makurdi. "I made a promise to God to be David's friend," she said. "I intend to keep it."

Her family members were not happy about this. They began to despise David. They counseled her that she had more than fulfilled her promise to him. She could maintain a long-distance friendship from any city with a postal service. Rita listened, but she felt that she must not leave David. The promise that she had made to God, and to David, would not let her simply get on with her own life. She came to work at Makurdi General Hospital where David lived.

At this time, however, she saw that the hospital was crippling him. She urged him to move out on his own. He did not want to leave, saying that he had no place to go. But she kept after him until he found a way to make it happen. He got a job with a pharmacy that had been willing to supply his drugs on credit. The owner had a one-room cabin that he could live in rent-free. Now he could begin to pay his own way, and repay at least some of his debt.

Rita continued to visit, bringing meals, and encouraging his faith in the Lord. A fine Christian man began to call on Rita at her home. Her parents were pleased with him as a potential husband for their daughter. She could see where this was headed and she cut it short. She told the man that there was no possibility of her marrying as long as she remained true to her promise to take care of David.

David learned about this, and was overcome with emotion. He had nothing to offer her, but one day he wrote, "Rita, will you marry me?"

She hesitated. "God will make it clear if we are to marry," she replied. "First of all, my parents would not approve. They are godly parents. They are the parents God has given me, and I believe I must have their approval and blessing." She became very thoughtful. "David, I think when you talk again, this will change everything. I believe you will talk someday."

David's heart fell. He wanted to believe that he would talk again, but he just couldn't. His trust in God had been fragile at best. Now it was broken. He continued to go back and forth in his mind between images of a God of love, and a God of fate. Too often, he forgot to count his blessings, and he hardly ever failed to count his curses. He became someone who was hard to love.

These were the longest years of his ordeal. His life became limited and defined by his disorder. Apart from his work at the pharmacy, much of his energy was devoted to endless attempts to collect his 1,000,000 naira from the woman who had hit him with her car. All of her delaying legal appeals were finally exhausted. The award had been upheld by the court. All that remained was to collect. He collected nothing.

He had the court intervene with her employer to attach her paycheck. About the time the attachment began, she was fired. She secretly took another job. When he discovered this, he tried the process again, and she repeated her pattern. In some ways, nothing had changed from the day she had hit him with the car. She was still avoiding responsibility. He was still being struck down. How could God allow it? How could He dangle one million naira in front of him – so close, yet so far away?

The woman declared hardship. If David had taken a hard line and had the police send her to jail, all hope of receiving anything from her would vanish. He was stuck, and he became worn out with chasing justice. All of his efforts to get the system to work for him were made worse by his handicap. He found few people, if any, who were patient with him in his inability to speak. As a final indignity, the government issued him a license to beg for a living. They too, had given up.

Meanwhile, Rita continued as always, checking on his condition, bringing occasional meals, running errands. She continued to encourage him in his spiritual life. She prayed with him often and took him to churches and crusades in Makurdi. She took him to Christian counselors. But he continued to struggle in his faith and his emotions. Up and down, up and down.

Eight long years passed. By now everyone who knew David, knew that his aphasia was a real disorder. Also, by this time David knew that Rita was a godsend, and he was totally unworthy of her. The example of her steady faith next to his wavering faith, became unbearable at times. He found a measure of relief during those times when they were apart.

I knew nothing of David and Rita's story when our team came to town. In February of 2003, Christ for all Nations held a crusade in Makurdi. A large field had been secured for our lights and sound systems. We were prepared to see crowds of 200,000.

When Rita heard about the meeting, she called David and urged him to go. She told him that in her Christian life, she had never seen a miracle, but she had heard that many miracles happened in our crusades. Our publicity posters promised that I would pray for the sick, as I always do. She did not go to the meeting with David. For some reason, she felt that this was something he must do on his own. Secretly, she was close to despair over his lack of improvement.

David also felt desperate. He was coming to the end of his ability to keep his promise to Rita, and he knew it. Thoughts of suicide were plaguing him again. Something had to change. Enough was enough. For one last time, he would seek healing from God. This time he would not put his trust in the doctors or medicine. He would not seek help from the courts or the government. He would fast and pray, asking God to heal him at the Bonnke crusade. Failing that, he would find a way to release Rita from her promise.

On our opening night in Makurdi, 180,000 people crowded the field. Thousands of sick people came close around the platform. David stood at the perimeter and counted his chances of being prayed for by Reinhard Bonnke at zero. At the end of the sermon, as I made a general prayer for the sick, he turned and walked away.

He should accept his fate, he thought. God did not care enough to heal him, and he would never be good enough to deserve it. Bonnke had faith for healing, but he did not. And God would not let him get close enough so that Bonnke could lay hands on him. He walked home and sat on his bed in the dark. The clock on his table glowed with the hour, 11 p.m.

He felt a trickle of warm blood begin to flow from his nostrils. He got up and found a towel to stop the flow. But it wouldn't stop. It continued for an hour, and then for another. He ran out of rags to stop the bleeding. As the third hour of bleeding began, he realized that he was dying. Perhaps his blood thinners had taken over.

He felt that he had one last chance to communicate. He had no telephone because he had no need for one. In the corner of his room was the latest binder Rita had prepared for his writings. He found his note pad and pen and began to write his last will and testament, leaving his few belongings to Rita. He expressed his love to her and his deep gratitude for her friendship.

Now she would be free of her promise to be his friend, he wrote, and she could go on and find a godly man to be her husband. He wrote that God would surely take good care of someone as faithful as her. He wrote that he would be free, too, and that he was ready for his ordeal to be over. With tears and blood falling onto the page, he said good-bye, signed his name, and dated it, February 3, 2003.

He left the door of his room open so that his body would be found in the morning light. Then, the young man who had struggled to lose his loneliness, lay down to die.

Another hour passed. The bleeding continued unabated. Strangely, David felt fine. Why wasn't he weak from the loss of so much blood? He got up and looked at his clock. It was 4 a.m. His nose was still flowing with a steady stream of blood.

He took his note pad from the desk and walked outside. The city was dark. Above him the stars filled the night sky. They stared down with cold indifference. If he had never lived, those stars would shine on. If he stopped breathing, they wouldn't care. They seemed too much like the God who made them.

He began to walk. As he did he began to sob, his shoulders shaking silently. He had never felt more alone. If ever he needed his voice, it was now. He would scream to the stars, "Why have You forsaken me?! Why?!" He came to a park bench and sat down as dawn began to glow in the east. He still could not control his weeping, or his nosebleed.

Around 5 a.m. someone on his way to work found him. His voice was filled with alarm. "What happened to you, sir?"

David realized that his shirt was soaked with blood. His face was a mess. This person would call the police. He pointed to his mouth and shook his head to let them know he couldn't speak. Then he wrote quickly on his pad, "It's just a nosebleed. I'm fine."

"Then why are you crying?"

David decided to tell the truth to this stranger. He wrote, "It seems that the Lord is forsaking me. Why would the Lord forsake me? Doesn't He care?"

"How do you know when God forsakes you?" the stranger asked.

Suddenly, David could see himself. He was sitting on this park bench because God had preserved him, not because He had forsaken him. He had been bleeding steadily for six hours, and he was still strong. He should have been unconscious by now, or even dead, but he could stand and walk. He still had energy. He could almost hear Rita's voice saying, "God loves you, David. He will never leave you nor forsake you." Those words from her mouth were so powerful because she embodied them beyond anyone he had ever known. He had no place to hide from God's care.

He bent down and wrote again, "No, I am wrong. God is not forsaking me. He has been good to me. I believe He will do something even greater for me. I must build up my faith."

He went home and discovered that the bleeding had stopped. He cleaned up and went to work. David longed to talk with Rita about his strange ordeal. She was his best friend, beyond all others. But he reconsidered. She had been through enough. He would finish this without her.

He asked his boss to call his cousin John, who was a Christian. He had moved to Makurdi in recent years, and knew about David's condition. John agreed to come to the pharmacy. David asked him to go with him to the crusade that night. He told John how the crowd was so thick that he needed help to get to the very front. He was determined to get to Bonnke. He would ask him to lay hands on him and pray for a miracle of healing. John agreed to help.

David then wrote out his prayer request for Bonnke to read. In order to verify his story, he took the medical documents and the government license to beg, awarded to him because of his condition. Surely with this information Bonnke would be moved with compassion to ask God to do something for him.

At 7 p.m., they came to the crusade grounds. David carried his Bible and note pad. Some of the crowd had been waiting all day. Together, David and John pushed their way toward the platform. It was a long and difficult struggle. But as I began to preach that night, they had made it all the way to the steps beside the platform. At the base of the stairs stood Jason Betler, a member of our team.

David poked him in the side to get his attention. He wrote on his note pad and placed it in front of him. "I have been unable to speak since an accident eight years ago. I want a personal appointment with Reinhard Bonnke. I want him to pray for me so that I can speak."

Jason could see that David felt desperate. His heart went out to him. "I'm sorry," he said, "but there are too many people here who want to see Reinhard. We cannot make a personal appointment for you. But if you stay, Reinhard will pray for all of the sick at the end of the meeting."

David did not want this. He wrote again that he wanted Bonnke to pray for him personally. In his mind, he was fighting against fate. He saw all of the people in the crowd as resigned to their fate. At the time of mass prayer, Reinhard would pray over the entire audience and God would heal only those He chose to heal. David wanted better odds than that. He wanted to storm Heaven's gates and ask, even demand, a healing from God. In his mind, if Reinhard, the man of faith, would pray for him, this would happen. In this way he thought that he would break through the grip of fate. But as he continued to try to persuade Jason to make an appointment, Jason continued to refuse.

This threw David back into a lifelong emotional pattern. The old pain of loneliness returned to his heart in full measure. As Jason refused to hear his request, so David felt, God refused to give him access to His healing power. But on this night, David thought, something in this familiar pattern had to change. Giving in to this self-focused feeling had only produced more suffering. He'd had enough of it. It was time to go a new way. He would go against his feelings and take a step of faith, believing that God still had his best interest at heart, even though he felt rejected.

He and John walked away about thirty yards into the crowd where Jason could still see them. Jason recalls that David was wearing a bright red shirt, and it was easy to keep track of him.

After the salvation prayer, I addressed the sick people in the crowd as I usually do. I asked them to place their hands on the part of their body that needed healing. Then I began to pray.

As Jason describes it, he saw David place his hand on the back of his head and immediately fall to the ground as if someone had cut him down.

David experienced what Jason saw, but in a much different way. His testimony is that he laid his hand on his head and felt the warmth of a strong light shining on him from above. He thought it was a crusade field light. Something told him to look at it. When he looked up, the light shot down around him. It was so powerful it drew him inside. He looked out of the shaft of light at his cousin, John. John obviously did not see the light because he was looking at the stage as normal. David tried to reach out and grab him by the sleeve to get him to look at the light, but he could not reach beyond the light. He took his note pad to write John a note, but his hands felt too weak to write a single letter. He felt strangely cut off from reality.

He looked at the other people around him. No one else seemed to notice the light either. He was alone in this experience, but he hardly felt lonely. He was alone with God, and he felt thrilled with His love. A hand came down through the shaft of light and touched the back of his head. It removed something. He immediately felt relieved of a great burden.

The light began to fade, and he found himself on the ground in the crusade meeting. How did he get there? He felt confused and wondered if he had really experienced this light, or if it had been a dream. He felt as if he was still in a dream. As he came more fully to his senses, he thought that maybe he had collapsed from the loss of blood, or from the lack of sleep, or even from the previous days of fasting – or from a combination of these things.

John quickly helped him to his feet. "What happened to you?" he asked.

David had no reply. He didn't even think of using the note pad. John went on talking, but David could not concentrate on his words. He was still overcome by the experience of the light, and the hand that had removed something from his head.

At this point Jason Betler reports that he saw David reach to the back of his head again and fall to the ground as if cut down. This was the very same action as before.

Once again, David experienced what Jason saw, but in a much different way. He said that suddenly the light came back. This time it was even more powerful. He looked again at his cousin John, but once again, John did not see the light. The hand returned, touching the back of his head. Once again it removed something, and David felt lighter. This time, however, he felt another sensation as well; he knew that he had received something from God. The light disappeared, and he found himself on the ground.

John helped him to his feet. He seemed baffled and just a bit angry. The crowd was surging all around them. People were praying intently with their hands raised. "Who pushed you down, David?" he asked. "Who did this to you?"

David looked at John and for the first time in eight years, a word in his head found the power to make his mouth respond. "Jesus," he rasped.

John's jaw dropped. He stared. "Did you say something?"

"Jesus," David repeated. He felt like he was glowing. It never entered his heart to say any other word than the precious name of the Son of God. "Jesus."

John gasped. "David, I heard you."

"Jesus, Jesus, Jesus," David repeated. He began to walk around saying it. It was a hoarse whisper, but it was a miracle. He stopped and looked at his cousin again, taking him by the shoulders. "Thank you, John," he said.

John grabbed him in a bear hug. "God has healed my cousin!" he screamed to the people around him. "God has healed him! He can talk for the first time in eight years!"

From the stage I asked those who had received healing to approach the platform. I wanted to share with that vast crowd what God had done that night. John rushed with David back to where Jason Betler stood. He told him that David had been unable to speak for eight years, since his accident. Now he was talking.

"Jesus," David repeated, tears streaming from his eyes. "Jesus."

Jason took him with John, up the steps to meet me on the platform. Once again John explained the background to David's story.

I spoke to the crowd, "This man, named David Attah, has not been able to speak for eight years," I said. There was a stir across the audience. I did not know that David was well known to many people in Makurdi. Some were recognizing him. I placed the microphone near to his mouth, "Let's hear David do something he has not done for eight years," I said. "Count with me, David. Say, 'one'."

"*One*," David rasped.

"Two."

"*Two*," he repeated.

"Three."

"*Three*."

"Four."

"*Four*."

Suddenly David dropped to his knees, weeping with gratitude. He was simply overcome, and did not have any idea how to thank God for His great gift of healing.

A few months later we returned to another city in the coastal region of Nigeria for a crusade. David came to see us. He was beaming from ear to ear, and spoke fluently now in a full voice. I invited him to the platform to tell his story. He gladly did so. Later he told us that the strength of his voice continued to return. He still lapsed into a whisper whenever his voice grew tired.

Months later we returned to another Nigerian city. David came again, and this time, no one could stop him from talking. His face bore a new light. He introduced us to a beautiful woman named Rita, his fiancée, he said. Seeing her, we could easily understand his joy.

I asked my crew to take them both aside and record their full story. That is when I learned that after his healing, Rita took David to see her parents. Rita's mother met them at the door. She knew David well, and was not happy to see him.

"Hello, Mother," he said to her, his face breaking into a wonderful smile.

Rita's mother's eyes grew wide. Her hands flew to her cheeks. "David? Did you speak?"

"Jesus healed me," he said. "God is so good!"

Rita asked her stunned mother if she could invite David inside. Her mother nodded. So many emotions were hiding behind her blank stare: shock, anger, frustration, resentment, confusion, and those feelings were made worse by a sense of guilt for having felt that way toward David – someone God had obviously loved so much.

Rita knew what to do next.

She led David by the hand into her house, and to her bedroom. There, she had a bookshelf. It was full of eight years of conversations. Until now, they had been her treasures. She began to pile the notebooks into his outstretched arms. She loaded her mother's arms too. When the shelf was empty, she led them to the back door and out into the yard. A burn barrel was placed there. She took the notebooks one by one and began dropping them into the barrel. Then she doused them with gasoline and tossed in a match.

As the books went up in flames, a flood of tears released from her soul. She took David in her embrace. "I want to hear you talk, David," Rita said.

"I am talking," he said.

"But never stop. Don't ever stop talking to me, David. Promise me."

"I promise," he said.

Today, Mr. and Mrs. David Attah attend Bible college in preparation for a lifetime of ministry. David's healing has become widely known in Nigerian medical circles, as well as in most churches in that region of Africa. David and Rita travel together and never miss an opportunity to tell what God has done for them.

So whose story is this? It is the story of David's healing and of Rita's promise, and more. It is the story of God's love. His love enables each of us to witness to His saving grace, and also to His healing power. May God receive all the glory.

I was struck to hear Rita say that before David was healed, she had never seen a miracle. I would have to disagree. For eight years, she became a human mirror of God's love. That too, was a miracle.

Genesis establishes the law of seedtime and harvest. This story reminds us that there is sometimes a long, long time between the two. After the seed falls into the ground and dies, we continue in faith – yes, even in wavering faith – believing that the seed of His Word will not fail to produce a bountiful crop.

CHAPTER
TWELVE

BREAKFAST ON THE BISMARK

I will call him Nathan, but he could be Natasha or Johann or Kersten. He is one of millions of men and women who have come forward to receive the Lord at an altar call. When numbers become so large, they lose their meaning. Sometimes I think we must find a way to speak of just one; one person out of millions. And so, I speak of Nathan.

He wanted a supervisor's job in his home town. His late father had held the position before him. He had idolized his father. He knew that if he filled his shoes, he could afford to marry his childhood sweetheart. He wanted the position so much that he cheated on a qualifying test and was caught. The disgrace was made known, his reputation ruined, his job lost. The engagement to the love of his life fell apart.

Nathan looked for new ways to succeed after his fall, but everyone knew his shame. No one seemed ready to give him a second chance. His life had become stuck in the muck of iniquity, and he had no one to blame but himself. This is the all-too-common story of sin.

But I did not know any of this, so how could I care about Nathan? What moves me is to know that the Holy Spirit is not limited the way that I am. He knew every detail of Nathan's failure, and He cared for him perfectly. He cares about all the "Nathans" in our world. No one is left out. We must believe this with all of our heart if we are to be true evangelists.

As this story begins, the efforts in the early years in Lesotho were behind me. No one thought of Reinhard Bonnke as a missionary anymore. I was known, above all, as an evangelist. I had formed Christ for all Nations in Johannesburg. This organization was to be the vessel for accomplishing God's vision for a blood-washed Africa. But my spirit was restless.

We were having powerful results. We were seeing decisions for Christ in the tens of thousands in the nations of Southern Africa. Stadiums were being filled. We had a big tent that we pitched, so that 10,000 could gather under one canvas. Many thousands more would crowd around the outside to hear the Gospel. But still, the restless feeling kept nagging on the inside of me. What could it mean?

One night I went to sleep and began to dream. In this dream, I wore a sea captain's uniform. I stood on the bridge of a great ship. I gripped the helm. I could feel the powerful vibrations from the engine room through the wheel in my hands. The deck moved beneath my feet as tons of water were displaced by this moving giant. The ship was a floating city. It seemed as large as the infamous German Bismark battleship of World War II.

I noticed, however, that the ship was not on the open seas where I would expect it to be. In my dream, I was guiding the ship upstream along the twisting course of an African river in the night. Peering ahead in the gloom, I could see a bend. Looking to each side, I saw that the banks were growing narrower as I passed upstream. I slowly realized that my great ship was doomed. It would never make it around that bend. We were in dangerous waters.

I looked to see if I could turn around to avoid disaster, but the channel had no room. There was no going back. The hair rose on the back of my neck as I realized that there was no going forward, either. Such a dilemma!

In my dream, I broke into a terrible sweat. Everything was at stake, and all so suddenly. My hands trembled on the wheel as I watched the huge ship move closer and closer to unavoidable disaster. In desperation, I cut the power to the engines. They fell silent, but I had acted too late. Our massive momentum carried us forward.

Suddenly, I heard the horrible sound of steel groaning and screeching against the rocks. Gaping holes were torn in the hull. The huge Bismark-sized battleship lurched to a stop as the narrow banks caught and held it fast in the African night. I stood riveted to the spot, swallowed up by the sound of the rippling current and the chatter of bush insects in the darkness.

I awoke to find my bed sheets soaked with sweat. No one had to tell me that I had just had a dream from God. But what did it mean?

"Lord," I cried, "what is it?"

"*The ship,*" the Lord said, "*is a picture of your organization, Christ for all Nations.*"

"Lord, will we get stuck?" I asked.

"*No.*"

I felt great relief to hear this. Still, I knew that we were in dangerous waters. I must carefully listen to what the Lord would say about how to avoid shipwreck.

"A great battleship needs more than firepower," I heard Him say in my spirit. *"It needs maneuverability."*

"Yes, yes," I agreed. I could still recall the terrible moment when I realized that I could not turn the ship around to avoid getting stuck. The entire ship, with all of its marvelous firepower, had become locked in an immovable position by two ordinary riverbanks.

"Your foundation is too narrow and too small," the Lord said to me. *"The battleship is fine, but I will widen the river for you so that you can pass. I will add prayer partners to Christ for all Nations. Every prayer partner will widen the river by one inch."*

Now I understood the restless feeling in my spirit. God had been warning me of trouble that I didn't know was there. In His great love and wisdom, He had given me His plan for avoiding disaster. All of my energies became focused now. In obedience, I would find ways to gather new prayer partners to widen the river.

I did not know, as I began this new direction, that Nathan's life had run aground in a much different way. His dreams of being a supervisor and a respected family man had been torn apart. His efforts to rise above his own shame continued to fail on every side. His family and friends had deserted him. His reasons for living had gone.

I did not see him as he took a butcher's knife from the kitchen drawer. Day after day, he had been thinking of ways to make the pain of his life end. He had read a book that described how others had slashed the veins in their wrists and had gone to sleep forever. This sounded like Heaven to him. Just to escape his ruined life.

I could not hear Nathan as he began to sob all alone in his bedroom, holding that knife to his wrist. My ears were filled with the sounds of an engine room on a great battleship. I was hearing myself repeat the words, "All Africa shall be saved." I was thrilled to feel the ship moving again on that continental river. My job was to guide Christ for all Nations to see a blood-washed Africa. I did not hear Nathan's cries – but the Holy Spirit did. And He cared for him in his agony as much as He cared to widen my river.

Someone told me to go to a breakfast. It was a meal sponsored by another evangelist. I went. What I saw opened my eyes. I saw that this man of God had invited people to a special meal at which he presented his vision and invited his guests to become prayer partners. The Holy Spirit spoke to me that I should do this same thing.

The finest hotel I could think of in Johannesburg was The Carleton. I wanted nothing but the best for my partners. We hired it for a breakfast. I sent out invitations to the finest Christian leaders in all of Southern Africa. I wanted them to come to a Christ for all Nations meal where God would widen my river.

And how they came! As I sat at the head table, my heart swelled with gratitude at the response. There was not an empty chair at any of the tables in that large ballroom. I looked across the faces of wonderful Christian leaders from all denominations and ministry organizations in the region. Some of my former critics were there – people who had said bad things about me, but now wanted to support our ministry. I saw Christian business leaders, politicians, pastors, friends, and ministry executives. Christ for all Nations has certainly become a great ship of evangelism, I thought, if it can enjoy the favor of this blessed crowd.

The breakfast was served to the guests, and a time of warm fellowship followed. I can still hear the wonderful hum of conversation in that room, mingled with the tinkle of glasses and silverware on plates. It moved me to know that all of this activity was leading to the presentation of a vision of seeing perhaps millions of souls saved through Christ for all Nations in the years ahead.

Then came the time for me to present the vision. I stood and walked to the podium. Again, my heart overflowed. I thanked my guests for coming. I let them know that it was an honor to know they cared enough to respond to our invitation to this breakfast. Then I presented God's plan for increasing our maneuverability. The time had come to ask them to consider joining us as prayer partners.

Suddenly, the Spirit whispered in my heart, *"Give an altar call."*

I stopped talking at the podium. Surely I had heard wrong. This was not a crowd of sinners. These were Christian leaders. They might be insulted if I gave an altar call for salvation. Or, if one in the room who had a great reputation was somehow still unsaved, that person would be exposed for his or her hypocrisy by responding in this public meeting.

"Give an altar call."

I heard the message clearly this time. No mistake about it.

"My friends," I said, "I have heard from the Holy Spirit that I should give an altar call. In a crowd like this, I must say, I did not plan to do this, but I will simply obey the Lord. Will you please bow your heads just now?"

There was a lot of clearing of throats in the room. There were coughs. You could hear the scraping of chairs and rustling of garments as the crowd of believers slowly bowed their heads. Now they waited in silence.

"I would like to ask everyone to examine themselves honestly this morning. If your life should end today, do you know where you would spend eternity? Do you have that certainty? If you have received Jesus as your Savior, of course, to be absent from the body is to be present with the Lord. But if you have not accepted Jesus as your Savior, then you have ignored the one gift of salvation that God Himself has provided for you. How can you escape if you reject so great a gift? I would like to ask those in this room who would like to accept Jesus as their Savior right now, to raise their hands."

In every altar call there is a moment of recognition for the audience. It comes when they have bowed their heads in prayer, and then hear the pastor or evangelist say, "Yes, I see that hand." These words mean that in the assembled group, someone is not saved, and that person has acknowledged it by raising his hand. He has made his private lost condition public. It would be fair to say that among these Christian leaders, each was highly curious to know if any of their number would respond. No doubt, they would be shocked if one hand was raised. And, frankly, so would I. You could hear a pin drop in that room as I asked for a show of hands.

"Yes, I see that hand," I said. "And you, and you, and you, and you, and another, and yet another. Yes, yes, yes, yes, yes… I see that hand." And still, there were more.

You could feel something like electricity ripple through the atmosphere. But what none of my Christian friends knew was that I was receiving a great revelation of God's love and grace. It was coming to me in a way I would never have imagined.

Each member of that crowd was, no doubt, asking him or herself, how could so many wonderful Christian leaders not know Christ as their Savior? Some in the audience even began to break from their positions of prayer to see who had raised a hand.

"This is a solemn moment," I said. "I ask that we remain in an attitude of prayer. The Spirit is speaking to many hearts here this morning. We do not want to miss what He is doing."

After another moment, I said, "I would now like to ask those who raised their hands to come forward and stand here in front of me. Do not delay. If you need to receive Jesus this morning, come now."

I will never forget it. Seventeen people came forward, some of them running. They quickly assembled in a line in front of that speaker's platform, some weeping, others trembling, all moved by the Holy Spirit to accept Jesus as their Savior.

Then I said to the crowd, "You may lift your eyes now, and see what God has done."

That crowd of Christian leaders raised their heads. Now they received the same revelation that had already come to me. Each of the seventeen persons standing in front of me wore a Carleton Hotel uniform. These were the people we had overlooked in our search for prayer partners. These were the servants, the waiters whom we had not counted in our minds as we had enjoyed our breakfast. Seventeen waiters wanted to know Jesus.

I looked at this crowd of Christian friends, and said, "Is this not why we came here? We should all go home today with the greatest of joy. By coming to this Christ for all Nations breakfast, we have helped to make these seventeen divine appointments possible."

Handkerchiefs appeared across the room. A holy silence had fallen. Nothing I could have said or done better illustrated the nature of our calling to be witnesses and evangelists of the Good News.

One young pastor was totally changed that morning. He vowed from that day forward that he would never address any group, anywhere, for any reason, and not give an altar call. Such evangelistic faithfulness will always bear fruit. In his case, his church eventually grew to encompass a congregation of 40,000 members in that city.

I went on to lead those seventeen waiters in the sinner's prayer. Then I greeted them, one by one, shaking their hands and letting them know that this was not the end of their relationship with the Lord – just the beginning.

I reached the last waiter in line, a young man. I took his hand.

"And what is your name?" I asked.

"Nathan."

"Nathan," I said, "welcome to the family of God."

He nodded and smiled at me with tears streaming down his face. He held my hand in both of his, and for a long time he just kept shaking it. He would not let it go. I could tell he was deeply moved. I didn't have time to ask, but I knew that a very long and important story lay behind this moment of decision in his life.

There is a story like Nathan's behind each of the millions of decisions for Christ that we register. Won't Heaven be wonderful? We will be given more than enough time to hear them all, from beginning to glorious end.

❧

We are not only agents of omnipotence, we are agents of omniscience. We don't have to know everything — God does. Trust His perfect knowledge. If we tune into His voice and obey it, He will see to it that we are used in His great purpose to plunder Hell and populate Heaven.

CHRIST
FOR ALL NATIONS

For further information about the ministry of Reinhard Bonnke or
Christ for all Nations, please visit our website on the internet or contact
the office nearest to you;

Christ for all Nations
P.O. 590588
Orlando
FL 32859-0588, USA

Christ for all Nations
P.O. Box 25057
London, Ontario
N6C 6A8. Canada

www.CfaN.org

Full Flame

For information about the purchase of other books and booklets by
Reinhard Bonnke contact;

Full Flame, LLC
P.O. Box 593647
Orlando, FL 32859
USA

www.FullFlameOnline.com